SELF-DIRECTED SYSTEMATIC DESENSITIZATION

a guide for the student, client and therapist

Wes W. Wenrich

NORTH TEXAS STATE UNIVERSITY

Harold H. Dawley

VETERANS ADMINISTRATION HOSPITAL
and TULANE UNIVERSITY SCHOOL OF MEDICINE
NEW ORLEANS, LOUISIANA

Dale A. General

NORTH TEXAS STATE UNIVERSITY

International Standard Book No.:
0-914-47418-9

Library of Congress Catalog Card No.:
76—9019

Printed and bound by:
Edwards Brothers
Ann Arbor, Michigan

Staff:
Design and Artwork: Michael Frazier
Editors: Elizabeth L. C. Wolf
Barbara E. Swart
Composer: Susan Wiltse
Mechanical Preparation: Sharon Sattler

To Frances Shellenberger Wenrich,

who views "life as just a bowl of cherries," has an insatiable penchant for thoroughbred horses and fox hunts, and assumes that everyone "summers" in East Hampton.

W.W.W.

To Linda Tell Dawley,

whose patient support and encouragement in this venture are deeply appreciated.

H.H.D.

To Cass,

who's given me light in many a dark moment.

D.A.G.

He who hath been bitten by a snake fears a rope.
— English Proverb

table of contents

ABOUT THE AUTHORS

Wes W. Wenrich

Dr. Wes W. Wenrich is an associate professor of psychology at North Texas State University where he teaches courses in behavior therapy, behavior modification, psychopathology, and related areas. Besides co-authoring the **Patient's Manual for Systematic Desensitization,** Dr. Wenrich has written the very popular **Primer of Behavior Modification,** and edited the text **Conditioning and the Modification of Maladaptive Human Behavior.** He has also published a wide variety of articles in the areas of reinforcement, behavior modification, and operant conditioning.

Harold H. Dawley

Dr. Harold Dawley is a staff psychologist with the Veterans Administration Hospital in New Orleans, Louisiana, and a lecturer in the Department of Psychiatry and Neurology at Tulane University. He is currently working in the area of behavioral treatment of smoking, obesity, sexual dysfunction, nonassertiveness, avoidance behavior, and related maladaptive disorders. In addition to contributing to the bestselling text, **Relax (How you can feel better, reduce stress, and overcome tension),** Dr. Dawley has co-authored the **Patient's Manual for Systematic Desensitization,** and **Achieving Assertive Behavior: A Guide to Assertive Training,** and has published over 30 papers and articles in the area of psychology and behavior therapy.

Dale A. General

Dale A. General received his B.A. degree from Western Michigan University in 1972, and is currently working toward a PhD degree in clinical psychology at North Texas State University where he serves as Systems Consultant and Advisor to the Behavior Exchange Clinic in the Center for Behavioral Studies. In addition to this text, he has co-authored two other books, **Introduction to the Concepts of Psychology,** and **Issues in the Analysis of Behavior,** and has worked as a staff writer, editor, and production manager of Behaviordelia, Inc.

PURPOSE

We have written this manual for two reasons: Our first was to provide step-by-step instructions on how people can deal with their learned fears or phobias through systematic desensitization. Toward this end, we've tried to lead our readers through this technique, acquainting them with its conceptual bases, looking toward the hassles involved in self-directed programs, giving hints to smooth their road to success. And our second purpose was to present this technique and its variations in a concise, readable way for clients, students, therapists, and anyone else wishing to learn about this area. So, you don't need any prior knowledge of psychological principles or concepts. All you need is the incentive to learn, and having learned, to act.

AUDIENCE

In view of our goals, we've aimed this manual at three kinds of readers — the client, the student, and the therapist.

To the Client

We've devoted the beginning part of this manual mainly to you, and to breaking your learned fears. The first two sections ("The Making of a Phobia," and "The Breaking of a Phobia") contain what you'll need to understand and design your own desensitization program, from start to finish. Appendix 1 consists of a variety of sample anxiety-stimulus hierarchies to use as models for your own. Appendix 2 contains a checklist that will help you keep track of your progress. We suggest you read these parts with care.

In the third part of the manual, we cover further aspects of systematic desensitization, outlining the history of its development, giving several variations people have used, and discussing areas where problems might arise. Reading this part will add to the first chapters in rounding out your knowledge of the technique.

We suggest that you use this manual with the help of a professional behavior therapist, although a highly motivated person could use it by itself. Not that a trip through self-modification requires a translator or "tour-guide". It's just that the therapist can assist your progress — giving you support, smoothing out rough spots, trouble-shooting your program as you go along, and using his or her skill with this technique to help make your experience a more rewarding one.

To the Student

We think you'll find this a worthwhile addition to your knowledge of behavioral techniques. The first part of the manual deals with the basic concepts in systematic desensitization, while the latter part covers its history, variations, and problems. We've also included references to books and articles to further expand your knowledge of the technique. We suggest you read the entire manual, and get a feel for the steps involved in the procedure, as well as its applications.

To the Therapist

Those of you already familiar with systematic desensitization, can use this manual in your therapy, perhaps saving you time in explaining the concepts, providing instructions for hierarchy design and deep muscle relaxation, and setting the stage for the desensitization process.

If you don't already know this technique, the manual will explain its bases, give complete guidelines on how to apply it, and prompt you (we hope) to look further into this way of dealing with anxiety. We suggest, of course, you read the entire manual before using it with a client.

STYLE

We've found people enjoy reading material containing some humor, and relating to real-life happenings. So, we've written in an informal style, avoiding the use of dry, overly-technical psychological jargon, shooting for clarity and relevance of the concepts, but not oversimplifying the material. We've tried to add some juice without making the meat soggy.

In our humble attempt at this (and much to our publisher's dismay) we've used "subjective" language at times. So, let us define our terms before the more technically-oriented of you bombard us with complaints about using such (profane?) language. By *pleasant* and *comfortable* we mean **rewarding** or **reinforcing**. In the same vein, we use *uncomfortable* to mean **aversive, negatively reinforcing**, or **punishing**. *Tension* refers to the verbal labeling of certain internal responses, such as physiological arousal, as does *feeling tense. Fear* and *anxiety* both mean the group of internal responses involved in physiological arousal to aversive stimuli. With all that clearly in mind, you should be ready to begin. We hope you enjoy the book.

A NOTE TO THOSE USING THIS MANUAL
FOR BEHAVIOR CHANGE

We would like to hear about the results you get using this manual. Please send any feedback or comments you may have, to the publisher. May a thousand reinforcers fall upon you good people for doing this. Thank you.

W.W.W.
H.H.D.
D.A.G.

section 1

the making of a phobia

chapter 1
anxiety and fear

THE ELEVATOR

"I know it's silly, Roger, but I can't get into that thing . . . you *know* that. Why do you keep insisting?"

"Margie, the lawyer's office is on the twenty-second floor! If we have to walk up the stairs it'll take the rest of the day. Please. Just try it. I'll be with you . . . really, there's nothing to be scared of. See? It's coming down now . . . c'mon, let's try it — just once, okay?"

"O . . . okay . . . I'll try . . . it's almost here. Oh, Roger, I can't do it . . . I *can't!*"

"Sure you can, honey. This is the safest elevator in the city. Here it is . . . let's just step right in here . . ."

"Let me out *please!* Roger, I'm getting sick! D . . . don't make me — I can't do it! Please . . . I can't breathe!"

"Okay, *okay!* Margie, I'm trying to be patient, but we've got to do something. You can't go on like this . . . you can't avoid elevators for the rest of your life . . ."

"I know, I-I know . . . I'm sorry, Rog, I really am. But I can't help it. You don't know what it's like . . . I-I can't help it . . ."

* * *

Margie and Roger Appleton. A couple with very few problems in their lives, except this one: Margie can't bring herself to get into an elevator. This didn't really matter where they used to live. But it sometimes creates problems since they've arrived in New York City. When faced with an elevator, Margie breaks out in a sweat, begins to tremble, and feels faint and nauseous. And, she can't help herself, in spite of all the trouble this causes them. Margie Appleton has an elevator phobia.

THE TV SET

John Klien shook his head sadly as he looked at his new TV set. *This is really absurd . . . I can't go through my whole life this way. Why can't I do it?*

He looked at the electric cord, moving his eyes slowly from the set, down the length of the cord to the large black plug on the end. The empty electrical outlet waited — silent, mocking.

John's eyes darted around the small room — looking for something — anything — to give him the strength, the power he needed to carry out the seemingly simple task at hand. He found nothing. He wished his roommate were home so the burden could be lifted from him. . .

"Hell with it," he said, "I'm gonna do it . . ."

His hand shook as he moved to pick up the snake-like TV cord. He pulled it slowly toward the outlet, closer and closer . . . But he dropped the cord suddenly from his hand, as if it had burned him. He ran into the kitchen and leaned against the counter, straining to calm the fear welling up inside. The outlet remained empty. John had failed again.

*   *   *

Like Margie with elevators, John has a "phobia" about electricity, a phobia that has grown to include electric devices of all sorts. They make him feel anxious and tense, even though he knows they can't really hurt him. He just can't bring himself to do much of anything that involves electric current. It causes him many problems, and he can't help it. John has an electricity phobia.

ANXIETY AND FEAR

What is anxiety? The activity involved in being anxious has been with us for a long time, actually. Nature has provided us with some amazing ways to adjust to our world through the course of our evolution. Not the least of these is a sort of "defense-alarm" arousal system. Under certain situations, like danger, this system leaps into action. Our heart beats faster. Blood pressure increases, adrenalin pumps into the blood, and many other physiological actions speed up. These reactions show the body's way of getting ready to "fight" or "run". We mobilize — prepare for instant action. A good thing too. This set of reactions can help keep us alive and kicking, and out of danger. We've all felt this surge of power in times of danger.

But, this arousal system can also get in the way. For instance, when there's no real danger. Sad but true, many people walk around fully mobilized and tense most of the time. All of the crises powers are reacting in the body, but there's nothing to fight and nowhere to run. We call this state of affairs **anxiety**. We also call it being up-tight, nervous, tense, wired, etc. But it all boils down to an aversive, disrupting sort of arousal. And, it often stops people from doing some of the things they want to do.

We may use the word "fear" when a specific event causes anxiety, as in Margie's **fear** of elevators. We use the term **anxiety** when the causes of the arousal are vague or unknown. This distinction isn't really important. Throughout this manual, we'll use fear and anxiety to mean the same thing — the set of responses involved in the emergency-arousal system.

IRRATIONAL FEARS AND PHOBIAS

We've all felt the icy fingers of fear grab us from time to time during our lives. Brushes with death or injury, diseases and painful experiences, all cause fear to varying degrees. And, being aroused in the presence of real danger helps us get by, as we've just seen.

But, what about a fear of being alone? Or of dogs, or meeting new people? Or heights, or harmless snakes? We often label the anxiety we feel in harmless cases, "irrational", or even "silly". After all, nothing here can really hurt us. When such persistent, unrealistic fears are caused by specific things or events we call them **phobias**. And these phobias are still disturbing in spite of any logical absence of danger. And they are just as hard to deal with.

For Margie Appleton, the prospect of getting into an elevator is just about as alarming as the cold barrel of a pistol pressed against her neck. And, for John Klien, the thought* of even a mild electric shock packs nearly as much fear as the thought of a head-on collision.

---

*Note: By **thought**, we mean covert verbal behavior, for the most part.

Many of us have unrealistic fears of one kind or another. They come in all shapes and sizes. We can live with many of these. We can avoid the objects causing the fear. Others may go away with time. But some are so strong, so powerful, they confound our daily life. Imagine a salesperson with a fear of meeting new people? A pilot with a fear of flying? Or a teacher with a fear of speaking in front of large groups? These reactions may remain a problem for months, years or an entire lifetime.

But, an important point is the fact that undue anxiety is a **learned** reaction. We weren't born with it. And, it most likely had its origin where it was suitable to fully mobilize. Also, being learned behavior, it can be *un*learned. Some very effective ways of reducing these types of fears have been developed. This manual deals with some of them. But, before we look at these, let's first take a look at where it all begins.

chapter 2
how to learn a phobia without really trying

A few years back, John and some friends were cruising the block on Halloween night, talking and laughing, dreaming up daring pranks to wreak upon the neighbors. In the midst of the "battle plan", John spotted a street lamp with its outer globe broken. The huge inner light bulb was exposed. . .

"Wouldja look at the size of that bulb? I gotta have it. . ."

"Really!" one of the others said. "But how're you going to get it down without getting fried? There's alot of juice up there, John . . ."

"Aw, it'll be a cinch, man . . . watch this . . ." John shinnied easily up the slick metal pole, and began to unscrew the bulb. One turn . . . two turns . . .

"AAAArrrggghhhh!"

A hot surge of city electricity pulsed through his body. He fell trembling to the ground, filled with arousal and anxiety, but otherwise unharmed.

UNLEARNED AND LEARNED FEAR STIMULI

Fear and anxiety don't just happen. Like other things we do, something causes them. The original arousal related to John's phobia was caused by a massive jolting dose of electricity. Many other things prompt intense arousal: extreme heat and cold, loud noises, other forms of physical harm. These and similar stimuli produce discomfort in an automatic way, due to the make-up of our body. They arouse us the first time we meet them; we don't have to learn to "fear" them. In other words, they are **unlearned stimuli** for fear.

When we contact unlearned fear stimuli, things coupled with them also come to cause arousal, where they didn't before. They become **learned** stimuli for fear. In John's case, the once "harmless" light bulb and lamp post were paired with the painful shock, and later produced a similar reaction (e.g., arousal). In the same way, after a person has a serious car accident, they will show fear arousal around cars, most likely, where once they didn't. Someone who's been bitten by a dog may become anxious around dogs, the dogs acquiring anxiety-producing properties themselves, through their pairings with unlearned fear stimuli.

Consider the following diagram showing how John learned to fear lamp posts and light bulbs. First, we have the unlearned fear stimulus of electric shock, which causes anxiety arousal:

electric shock ──────────⟶ arousal

But also present at the scene were the light bulb and the lamp post:

light bulb
lamp post
electric shock ──────────⟶ arousal

And although they were neutral or harmless at first, as a result of this pairing they became capable of causing the same sort of arousal that the shock produced (but now in the absence of shock):

light bulb ──────────⟶ arousal
lamp post ──────────⟶ arousal

They've become **learned fear stimuli.**

This type of learning isn't limited just to pairings with unlearned, or harmful stimuli. If a learned fear stimulus is paired with a neutral one, new learned fear stimuli will result. To illustrate this concept, let's flash back into the life history of Margie Appleton.

***

Margie, aged five, somehow locked herself in a closet while playing. Her eyes explored the small, dark area. It was totally black, except for the thin slit of light seeping under the door. *They'll be by soon,* she thought, *any minute now . . .* She listened intently for the slightest sound from the outside world, waiting for what seemed like hours, but could have been only seconds. There were no sounds. She began to worry.

What if they never come? What if I die in here before they find

me? What if I use up all the air in here and can't breathe? I'm gonna die in here before someone finds me! Her thoughts raced ahead, imagining the worst things possible. She started to cry out, loudly, banging the door with her small fists.

Her parents found their terrified child a few moments later, after hearing the uproar. They soothed and calmed her, and wondered what it was about the "harmless" closet that could have scared her so much.

Here we have a child, trapped by accident in a closet — at one time a fairly neutral, harmless stimulus. While in the small room, she became fearful of never being found, of dying there. She thought and lived some very punishing things. The thoughts (which function as learned fear stimuli) were paired with the closet, causing this high level of fear arousal. And like the light bulb and lamp post in John's case, the once harmless closet now caused arousal in its own right, through learning. Now, every time Margie finds herself in an enclosed space, the arousal linked with her early bout with the closet returns. The phobia has begun.

So, you see, the causes of unfounded fears lie in unlucky, and often accidental pairings of fear stimuli with neutral stimuli. And these quite often involve learned fears to begin with. Actual contact with unlearned fear stimuli isn't made in many cases. Take a fear of flying, for example. How many people with this fear have actually been hurt in some way related to plane accidents? Not many. But flying in a plane while imagining a crash may result in pairing a lot of fear and anxiety with flying. Result? Planes and flying become capable of causing arousal.

But, how can thoughts cause anxiety? How do they become fear stimuli? Thoughts are, for the most part, verbal — words, cues, things we say to ourselves. So, one of their functions is that of a stimulus. And, like any other kind of stimulus, thoughts can take on a learned fear-producing function as a result of being paired with fear stimuli. Let's take a simple example to illustrate what we mean — the word "pain". "Pain" is often paired with aversive, arousing stimulus events throughout our lives, as we grow and experience, events which for the most part are unlearned fear stimuli:

> "pain"
> unlearned fear stimuli ——————⟶ arousal

As a result, this word, or thought, comes to cause arousal on its own, now as a **learned** fear stimulus:

"pain" ——————————⟶ arousal

Now, when this type of "loaded" thought is paired with a once neutral event — such as flying, or sitting in a dark closet — further learning takes place, resulting in the neutral stimulus also becoming a learned fear stimulus:

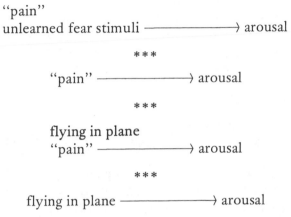

"pain"
unlearned fear stimuli ——————————⟶ arousal

* * *

"pain" ——————————⟶ arousal

* * *

flying in plane
"pain" ——————————⟶ arousal

* * *

flying in plane ——————————⟶ arousal

So, we have, in essence, a "second order" pairing going on in this situation, the neutral stimulus taking on fear-causing properties through pairing with the thoughts, themselves learned fear stimuli. This is a simple example, but you can see how quickly things get complex, each word and group of words having its own unique history of pairings within each person.

GENERALIZING LEARNED FEARS

But the learning story involves more than this. After the affair with the street lamp that fateful Halloween night, John was wary of trying the stunt again. And had the caution stopped there, it wouldn't be a problem. But it didn't. In a short time, he began showing anxiety around other things as well. Like appliances, outlets, extension cords — in short, nearly everything connected with electricity. Now the fear *was* a problem, because it interfered with his doing the things he needed to do to get by. It began affecting his day-to-day life.

In the same way, Margie's fear didn't stop with being locked in closets. She became fearful in small rooms, closed-in spaces, and, as we saw, elevators. This shows a very important property of learned fears. Once a stimulus acquires the power to cause fear, things and events similar to it in some way also come to produce the anxiety. And, this happens **even though these situations have never been paired with the original fear-producing stimulus.** When learned effects spread to stimuli like the stimulus present when the learning took place, we call it **stimulus generalization.**

Stimulus generalization is probably the main reason learned unrealistic fears persist. Once learned in one situation, the anxiety begins to occur also under conditions like the first: John's original fear of light bulbs generalized to all electric appliances; Margie's anxiety generalized from locked closets to all enclosed, small spaces. A child who's been attacked by a particular dog may then be aroused by all dogs, or even all furry, four-legged animals.

AVOIDANCE AND FEAR STIMULI

But, if a stimulus can acquire the power to cause anxiety by being paired with actual fear stimuli, won't it lose this power if it's no longer paired with them? If nothing happens to him when John comes in contact with electric appliances, won't they lose their learned ability to cause anxiety? Indeed they will. The trouble is, John won't seek out these objects. And, you won't find Margie hanging around elevators either, the very simple reason being that stimuli that cause anxiety also cause us to **avoid** them. So, the person never has the chance to be in the presence of the stimulus when it doesn't lead to harm. Even if it's never again paired with actual harm, the learned stimulus retains its power to arouse, as a result. The learned anxiety is never *un*learned. This, then, prevents most phobias from going away "by themselves". People avoid the learned fear stimuli, just as they do unlearned ones. And, as long as they're avoided, they retain their fear-producing functions.

So we see a simple but sometimes unfortunate learning pattern. Fear becomes coupled with a stimulus, an object, scene, or person, as the result of an arousing, aversive experience. Learned fear stimuli become ingrained. This fear spreads to other situations and stimuli like the first, and is then kept alive by the person's avoiding these situations. Avoidance is rewarded because it decreases the anxiety response, but at the same time makes the "unlearning" of the fear difficult or impossible. The result: the learned fear stimuli retain their power to cause anxiety and arousal, full-blown, in all their glory.

But there is a key to breaking this pattern: it's to remember that these fears are **learned**. Their causes are many and varied. They involve, as we've seen, unlearned and learned fear stimuli, along with all sorts of aversive experiences, both real and imagined. Luckily, we don't really need to know the exact cause of a specific phobia to deal with it. The techniques we discuss later deal more with reducing the anxiety than finding its exact cause. In some cases — like John's — the original pairing is obvious. In others, it may have been forgotten. In still others, no one knew it in the first place.

The point is that being learned, these fears can be unlearned. The presence of unfounded fears doesn't mean you're insane, crazy, mentally ill, or even whacked-out. It simply means you've had some unlucky learning experiences, whether you were aware of them at the time or not. And, some very effective techniques have been found to help you reduce these fears. In the pages that follow, we'll look at how they work.

section 2
the breaking of a phobia

chapter 3
systematic desensitization

You learned your irrational fears, now you have to unlearn them, and replace them with other, more rewarding experiences. This won't be easy; since in many cases your fears have been with you a long time. But, with patience and motivation, and perhaps the help of a behavior therapist, you'll be able to reduce your anxiety to a great extent, if not get rid of it altogether. The technique we present in this book won't cure every ache and pain that may plague you. But, to the extent that your problem involves learned fears, it offers one of the best solutions available.

Systematic desensitization replaces anxiety with a different response, like relaxation. Quite simply, you work toward getting rid of your fear by learning to relax instead. This involves a three-step process:

1. Building anxiety-stimulus hierarchies
2. Learning deep muscle relaxation
3. Visualizing scenes from your hierarchy while deeply relaxed.

In the pages that follow, we'll discuss the three steps in detail, and include instructions, exercises, and hints to help you carry out the procedure. But, before we study them, let's take a brief look at each of the steps to give you an overview of what we'll be doing.

BUILDING ANXIETY-STIMULUS HIERARCHIES

Systematic desensitization exposes a relaxed person to a graded series of imagined scenes relating to their specific fear. You imagine yourself in a variety of aversive situations while trying to remain as relaxed as you can. Generally, you do this step by step. You begin with scenes causing little or no anxiety, and gradually move toward those scenes holding the most fear, rather than jumping into the worst scene you can imagine, right away. We call this ordered series of scenes an **anxiety-stimulus hierarchy.**

You'll design your own personal hierarchies — as they apply to whatever fears *you* have — ranking and ordering the scenes as you prepare for the actual desensitization process.

DEEP MUSCLE RELAXATION

Relaxation plays a major part in desensitization. Most of us relax at one time or another during the day, whether over a cup of coffee, sitting down in the evening to watch TV, going to a movie, or listening to music. Different people relax in different ways. But the type of relaxing we're talking about here involves more than just this. It involves a state marked by a complete lack of muscle tension, and by feelings of calm and peace.

Deep muscle relaxation helps in many ways. It helps reduce many problems resulting from intense or long-lasting states of fear, anxiety, grief, anger, and similar reactions. When we're anxious, our heart beats faster, our blood pressure increases, adrenalin pumps into our blood, and a host of other physiological actions occur. So, one of the first things we must learn in conquering anxiety is to control these responses, and relax fully. Deep muscle relaxation slows the heart rate, lowers blood pressure, and results in less of a strain on our bodies, for the most part. And, in today's fast-paced world, the healthful soothing feeling of being completely relaxed is something we can all enjoy and benefit from.

We've included a series of exercises that involve tensing and relaxing the muscle groups of the body you need to, to relax deeply. You'll have to apply a little effort, and a lot of practice, in learning them. Some of you will find it easier than others. But it's worth the effort to learn, both for desensitizing yourself, and for the fringe benefit of being able to relax totally whenever you want.

VISUALIZING THE HIERARCHY SCENES

You'll be ready to begin the actual desensitization process once you've built the hierarchies for your fears, and learned to relax deeply. This involves replacing your anxiety to scenes, with relaxation.

First, you must relax completely. Once there, begin imagining the first scene of your hierarchy, while you enjoy the rewarding relaxed state. If no anxiety occurs, you'll move on to the next scene and visualize it, again concentrating on remaining totally relaxed.

If at any time you feel anxious, you'll be instructed to stop thinking about the scene, and relax deeply again. Once you achieve this, you'll try again to imagine the scene without fear-arousal.

In this way you'll proceed through the entire hierarchy until you can imagine all the scenes without anxiety. This may take anywhere from 10 to 15 or more "sessions", depending on, among other things, how intense the fear is, how well you've designed your list, and how clearly you're "seeing" the scenes.

A NOTE ON VISUALIZING

The ability to imagine the specific scenes clearly and easily, is important for this technique to work. It's based on the notion that you react to imagined scenes in much the same way that you react to real-life events. Many of you will find you can imagine or "see" things pretty easily. But those who can't do this right off, can develop it with practice. Before beginning self-directed desensitization, you should check yourself out to see how well and how quickly you can bring, hold, and "stop" images and scenes. If you can imagine scenes rapidly and clearly, as well as stop them under your own control, this part of the process shouldn't cause any problems. But, if you do have trouble, take time out and practice. A little practice, along with the support and guidance of your therapist will most likely do the trick.

If you can't imagine clearly after a great deal of practice, your therapist can help you. Among other things, he or she may try graded real-life exposures, or other forms of the basic technique more suited to your problem. (For variations of this procedure, see the section on in-vivo and in-vitro desensitization.)

Now that we've briefly reviewed the bases of systematic desensitization, you're ready to begin the real thing.

chapter 4
how to build your own anxiety-stimulus hierarchy

TYPES OF HIERARCHIES

Anxiety-stimulus hierarchies are lists of scenes that involve events related to your specific fears. They begin with scenes causing little or no anxiety, and progress to those causing a great deal of anxiety. In this section, we'll look at some of the distinct types of hierarchy designs, followed by step-by-step instructions for developing your own.

Most hierarchies fall into two classes: those involving distance in time or space from a feared object or event, and those involving a specific theme the anxiety focuses around.

Distance Hierarchies

One of the most common ways of listing fear scenes is to rank them according to distance in space or time from the phobic object. For instance, a hierarchy for a spider phobia may begin with a scene placing the person far from the insect. From there the scenes gradually bring the spider closer and closer, until it actually touches the person. In the same way, a hierarchy for a fear of exams may begin with someone thinking about a test a month away, and end with thinking about actually taking the exam.

A good example of this kind of hierarchy is the following one for fear of looking out a window of a tall building.

1. Walking onto the first floor of a tall building.
2. Going to the window on the second floor and looking out.
3. Looking out of the window from the third floor.
4. Looking out of the window from the fourth floor.
5. Looking out of the window from the fifth floor.

6 Looking out of the window from the sixth floor.
7. Looking out of the window from the seventh floor.
8. Looking out of the window from the eighth floor.
9. Looking out of the window from the ninth floor.
10. Looking out of the window from the tenth floor.
11. Looking out of the window from the eleventh floor.
12. Looking out of the window from the twelfth floor.
13. Looking out of the window from the thirteenth floor.
14. Looking out of the window from the fourteenth floor.
15. Looking out of the window from the fifteenth floor.
16. Looking out of the window from the sixteenth floor.
17. Looking out of the window from the seventeenth floor.
18. Looking out of the window from the top floor.
19. Being on the top floor, window open, leaning over and looking out.

Theme-Oriented Hierarchies

This type of sequence involves changing different parts of the theme or situation which causes the anxiety, beginning with points that cause little fear, and moving to those producing the most anxiety. Think of a hierarchy for a fear of public speaking, for instance. The type of audience present, as well as its size, has a lot to do with the amount of fear produced, in this kind of phobia. So, the "quality" or type of people present in the scenes may begin with children or close friends, moving to other kinds of people, then perhaps to a group of professionals in the area the person is speaking about. Another example is the following hierarchy for a fear of being watched, in which the number and kinds of people watching the person vary throughout the scenes.

1. Walking outside of your house and saying hello to your neighbors.
2. Walking down the street and exchanging greetings with the postman.
3. As you walk by a large crowd of people waiting for a bus, you trip and they stare at you.
4. As you walk into a crowded supermarket, you notice that the people waiting to be checked out are staring at you.
5. In the supermarket as you're trying to pull out a grocery cart that's stuck, everyone is watching you.

6. You drop a large jar of pickles, and everyone in the store stares at you.
7. Walking into a large crowded department store, you drop your coat and all of the other people in the store stare at you.
8. When you're checking out in a crowded line, the clerk overcharges you. You bring this to his attention as the crowded line watches.
9. You're at work, and several fellow workers are standing behind you and watching you work.
10. Your boss joins a gathering of fellow workers, and they're all watching you work.
11. You make a mistake at work, with your boss bringing it to your attention. There is a crowd of fellow employees looking on, and they're laughing.

Mixed Hierarchies

Hierarchies often combine distance *and* theme-oriented items. Mixed hierarchies may be the most frequent type, perhaps because they're flexible in showing different dimensions of the particular fear involved. Consider the following fear of dentists hierarchy, for example.

1. You're on the way to the dentist's office.
2. You walk into the dentist's office.
3. You're seated in the dentist's waiting room and waiting your turn.
4. Your dentist walks by and says, "Hello."
5. You get up and walk into the dentist's examining room and are seated.
6. The dentist looks into your mouth.
7. The dentist checks all of your teeth.
8. The dentist starts probing your teeth with a hand instrument.
9. The dentist begins scaling your teeth with a hand instrument.
10. The dentist begins to clean your teeth.
11. The dentist bears down hard and your gums begin to bleed a little.
12. Your gums bleed more as the dentist continues to clean your teeth.
13. The dentist starts probing teeth for a soft spot.
14. She finds a soft spot and begins to probe deeper.
15. The dentist then uses the electric drill to bore out a soft spot in your tooth.
16. Drilling continues.
17. She has finished drilling your tooth, and then cleans out your mouth and begins to fill your cavity.

18. She locates a decayed tooth and tells you that she's going to extract it.
19. The dentist begins to extract your tooth.
20. You have a great deal of difficulty and discomfort as she extracts your tooth.

The first items deal mostly with distance, in terms of time away from the appointment, while the latter ones involve theme items, describing the dentist's actions and the person's reactions to them.

In truth, almost as many types of hierarchies exist as there are fears. Each one has to be custom fitted to the person and fears involved. We've included several sample hierarchies for you to look over in Appendix 1. They involve many fears, and include the types of items we just discussed. Read these over once or twice to get familiar with them before you begin to build your own list. You may well find one that relates to your specific fear. If so, use it as a model for your own hierarchy.

STEPS IN WRITING YOUR OWN HIERARCHIES

You should have some idea as to what's involved in writing them now that you've read about some of the different types of hierarchies, and looked at several examples.

First, write your irrational fears down on a piece of paper. Look at the list and see if some resemble others. Like a fear of crowds, and a fear of public speaking. A group of similar specific fears may, in truth, be the result of a single larger fear. For instance, the two fears we just mentioned could be related to a more general fear of being in a large group of people. If so, we can design a single hierarchy involving the larger fear rather than two lists relating to the specific fears.

Having chosen your fears and grouped them together, pick the one that's causing you the most trouble right now. If you're a salesperson with a fear of meeting new people, for instance, this is probably the one you'll want to work with first. Now with pencil, paper, and fear in hand, do the following:

Step One: Describe the Fear

Write a brief description of the specific problem you're going to work with at the top of a blank sheet of paper.

Step Two: List Fear-Producing Scenes

List all the situations relating to your fear that cause arousal. Let's use John's fear of electricity as an example. Some scenes would involve turning on electric appliances, or, even more aversive, plugging a cord into an electric outlet. Receiving a small shock would be extremely fear producing.

Make sure to describe the scenes clearly and in detail in doing this. Later on, you'll imagine these scenes, and it's important to be able to do this easily. The more detailed and vivid you make your scenes, the better you'll be able to visualize them later.

And don't leave any out that you can think of. If you feel later you have too many scenes to work with, you can delete some then. But for now, try and get all of those you can think of down on paper.

Step Three: Rank the Scenes

Once you've listed all the possible conditions linked with your fear, you'll need to rank and order them according to how anxious they make you. A good way to do this is to assign "subjective units of disturbance" (suds) to each scene. In this technique (developed by Wolpe and Lazarus, 1966) you give each scene a score value, ranging from 0 to 100 suds. A score of 0 suds refers to *no* anxiety being produced, while 100 suds means imagining the scene causes *extreme arousal.*

So, for John, sitting and listening to a radio would probably be close to 0 suds. Plugging in a radio may be rated as high as 75 to 80 suds, while receiving a small shock might be scored 100 suds.

Using the suds technique, assign a value to each of the scenes you've listed in the last step. After you finish this, take another sheet of paper and relist the scenes in order of their suds values. Begin with the lowest score, and proceed to the highest scene. You've now got your first rough anxiety-stimulus hierarchy.

Step Four: Put on the Finishing Touches

Now, smooth out your hierarchy, and put on the finishing touches. You should have roughly the same suds difference between the scenes in the hierarchy for the best results. In other words, don't have a scene fairly low in suds followed by one that's high. A good difference to have between scenes at the beginning of the sequence is about 10 suds. Toward the end, when the scenes are more disrupting, it may be best to have smaller differences between items (5 suds or less). If you have a large gap in suds between items, design scenes that will fit in that space, and add them to your hierarchy.

You may have any number of scenes in your finished hierarchy. But, a list that's too short might not work as well as a longer one. Also, a list that's too long may be pretty hard to work with. Most often, a hierarchy has 10 to 30 scenes in it, 20 being a good mean.

Look over your hierarchy with these points in mind. You may need to add or delete scenes to meet these guidelines. And, don't despair if your first hierarchy doesn't look perfect. Just try again. The first is the hardest. A point to remember: a poor hierarchy may mean poor results. You'll find the time you spend designing a good list will be well worth it later on.

Step Five: Stack the Deck

With your finished hierarchy shining brightly before you, list each scene on a separate 3 x 5 index card. Arrange a "deck" of these cards with the least anxiety-producing scene on top, and the one with the highest suds level on the bottom. This will make the scenes easy to reach during the actual desensitization procedure, allowing you to be a bit more flexible in changing, adding, or deleting items as you go through your program.

After you've finished these five steps, go over your hierarchy with your behavior therapist. If it's approved, you deserve a round of applause. If it isn't, work your way back through the steps until you've solved the problems. Once you've gotten your hierarchy under your belt, you're ready for the next step: relaxation training.

chapter 5
muscle relaxation exercises

The basic idea of these exercises* is to teach you how to relax fully. Studies have shown that a good method of doing this involves tensing the various muscle groups of the body as tightly as you can, holding and concentrating on the tension for a few moments, and then releasing it and noting the change. While tensing any one area of your body, the rest of your muscles should remain as relaxed as possible. As you go through the exercises that follow, you'll learn to enjoy relaxing more and more as the feeling becomes deeper and more complete.

You'll notice a series of three dots (. . .) throughout the exercises. These indicate periods where you should pause for five to ten seconds and concentrate on the sensations you're feeling at that time. If you can use a tape recorder, you should record these exercises and pauses. Then simply play back the tape and relax; otherwise, reading them will suffice.

You should practice twice each day. As you become used to the exercises, and better able to relax, you'll find some of the exercises can be combined and still produce the same effect. After a while, you should be able to relax fully in about five to ten minutes.

GENERAL LOOSENING UP

These exercises are designed to loosen up your major muscles, and they'll take about two or three minutes.

 ▪ Start by standing up and stretching your hands over your head as high as you can. Stretch all of the muscles from your finger tips

*These exercises are based on the work of Joseph Wolpe and Arnold Lazarus in *Behavior Therapy Techniques: A Guide to the Treatment of Neuroses*, New York: Pergamon Press, 1966.

down to your toes. Hold this tension for a few moments . . . then re-lax . . . Repeat this exercise several times.

▪ Now stretch your arms out sideways as far as you can, and tense them. Hold this tension for a few moments . . . then relax . . . Repeat this step several times.

▪ Now bend forward, tensing the muscles along your back and legs . . . study the tension for a few moments . . . then relax and notice the change . . . Repeat this exercise several times.

▪ Next shake your hands and arms lightly for a few seconds; re-lax all the muscles you can. Then sit down in a comfortable, reclined, lounge chair and do the following exercises.

RELAXING YOUR HANDS, ARMS, AND SHOULDERS

These exercises will relax the muscles in your hands, arms, and shoul-ders. They'll take about four to six minutes to complete.

You should already be seated with both feet extended out in front of you in a comfortable way, your arms and hands resting along the arm of the chair, and your head and neck in a relaxed, resting position. Relax like this for a few moments . . .

▪ Now, tighten your right hand into a fist, clench it as hard as you can, and build up the tension in your hand and forearm . . . Study this tension for a few moments . . . Now relax and notice the differ-ence . . .

▪ Once more, clench your right fist as tightly as you can, build up the tension, study it . . . Now relax and note the difference . . .

▪ Now, clench your left hand into a tight fist. Make the fist tighter and tighter, build up the tension and study it for a few moments . . . Relax and notice the difference . . .

▪ Once more, make your left hand into a tight fist, build up the tension in your hand and forearm tighter and tighter, study this ten-sion for a few moments . . . and now relax and feel the difference . . . Note how relaxed your hands are and how much more rewarding re-laxing is compared to tension. Concentrate on relaxing all over for a few moments . . .

- Next, bend your right elbow, making your right hand into a fist and tensing your forearm and upper arm as tight as you can. Build up this tension tighter and tighter, study it for a few moments . . . Now relax . . . straighten your arm and let the tension go . . . Feel the difference between being tense and relaxing . . . Enjoy the relaxed feeling for a few moments . . .
- Now, once more, bend your right elbow. Make your right hand into a fist and build up the tension in your hand, forearm, and upper arm. Build up this tension and study it for a few moments . . . Now relax . . . straighten out your arm and hand and let all the tension go. Spend several seconds comparing the feelings of your relaxed and tense muscles . . . Now, breathe normally and rest for a few moments . . .

- Next, bend your left elbow making your left hand into a fist, while tightly tensing your forearm and upper arm. Build up the tension in your upper arm, study it . . . Now relax and note the change . . . Notice how good it feels not to be tense . . . Enjoy this relaxed state for a few moments . . .
- Now, once again, bend your left elbow very hard, making your left hand into a tight fist and your upper arm muscle into a tight ball. Build up the tension as much as you can . . . Study that tension . . . Now relax and note the change . . . Let all the tension leave your muscles . . . Concentrate on relaxing as deeply as you can and remain that way for several seconds.

RELAXING YOUR NECK, FACE, AND SHOULDERS

These exercises will relax the muscles in your neck, face, and shoulders, and will take four to six minutes. Take a few moments and continue to rest.
- Now let your head roll slowly around for a few turns as loosely as you can . . . Next, turn your head to the right as far as you can, building up the tension and studying it . . . Now relax and notice the change . . . Note how good it feels to relax . . .
- Now repeat this step once more. Turn your head to the right as far as you can, build up the tension and study it for a few moments . . . Now relax and note the change . . .

- Next, turn your head to the left as far as you can . . . build up the tension and study it . . . Now relax and let all the tension flow out. Concentrate on the change . . .

• Once again, turn your head to the left as far as you can, build up the tension, study it . . . Now relax and note the change . . .

• Now, bend your head forward and press your chin against your chest as tightly as you can. Build up the tension . . . study it . . . Now relax and notice the change . . .

• Next, think about relaxing your shoulders. Begin by shrugging, or bringing your shoulders up as tightly as you can. Hold the tension for a few moments . . . Now relax and notice the difference . . .

• Repeat this step again. Shrug your shoulders as tightly as you can, build up the tension, study it . . . Now relax and feel the change . . . Relax all the muscles in your neck and shoulders . . . Relax all over as fully as you can . . . Continue relaxing for a while . . .

• Now, think about relaxing your facial muscles. Begin by frowning and wrinkling your brow as tight as you can. Build up the tension . . . study it . . . Now relax and notice the difference . . .

• Once more, frown and furrow your brow as hard as you can, build up the tension . . . study it . . . Now relax and note the change . . .

• Next, close your eyes and squint as tightly as you can. Build up the tension . . . study it . . . Now relax and notice the change . . .

• Once again, close your eyes and squint them tightly, build up the tension . . . study it for a few moments . . . Now relax and note the feeling . . . Let all the muscles in your forehead, around your eyes, and all over your face and entire body relax as fully as you can . . .

• Move on to your lips and tongue. Relax your lips by first pursing them tightly. Build up the tension, study it . . . Now release the tension and relax . . . Note the difference . . .

• Once more, pucker your lips tightly, build up the tension . . . study it . . . relax and notice the change . . .

• Now press your tongue against the roof of your mouth. Build up the tension and study it for a few moments . . . Now relax and notice the difference . . .

▪ Once more, press your tongue tightly up against the roof of your mouth . . . build up the tension . . . study it . . . Now relax and feel the change . . . Notice how much better you feel when you relax, and the tension is gone . . .

▪ Now, concentrate on relaxing all the muscles in your neck, shoulders, and face . . . release all the tension . . . Relax deeper and deeper . . . Continue relaxing for a while . . .

RELAXING YOUR UPPER BACK, CHEST, STOMACH, AND LOWER BACK

These exercises will last four to six minutes.

▪ Keeping the rest of your body relaxed, tense the muscles in your upper back area by raising your shoulders and shrugging them back and up. Tense them tight, build up the tension . . . study it . . . Now relax.

▪ Drop your shoulders and relax as completely as you can . . . Notice your upper back muscles relax . . . Relax more and more as the feeling spreads through your entire body . . .

▪ Now, once again tense the muscles in your upper back area by shrugging your shoulders up and back. Build up the tension . . . study it . . . Now relax. Let your shoulders fall, and, as they do, relax . . . Release all the tension . . . Concentrate on this feeling . . . Think about reducing even the least bit of tension . . . Continue to relax and enjoy this feeling for a few moments . . .

▪ Now, as you relax, breathe in deeply, fill your lungs as full as you can, and hold your breath for a moment . . . Breathe out slowly and notice the increasing relaxation . . . Breathe normally for a few seconds while you think about relaxing more . . .

▪ Breathe in deeply, and again fill your lungs completely, then hold your breath for a few moments . . . Now, exhale and let the air leave your lungs slowly. Concentrate on the increasing relaxation as you slowly exhale . . . Breathe normally for a while. Let yourself become more and more relaxed . . . Enjoy this spreading feeling as you breathe in and out . . .

▪ Once again, breathe in deeply, fill your lungs, and hold your breath for a few moments. Study the sensation . . . Now exhale slowly, and concentrate on the pleasant feeling as you do . . . Breathe normally again for a while, each time letting yourself become more and more relaxed . . .

▪ Once more, breathe in deeply and fill your lungs fully; hold your breath for a few moments. Study the tension . . . Now exhale slowly, think about relaxing more and more . . . Let this feeling spread through your entire body . . . Your upper and lower back, shoulders, neck, face, chest, and arms are all becoming more and more relaxed as you breathe . . . Think about relaxing more and more as you continue breathing. . . .

As the relaxation goes deeper and deeper, center you attention on your stomach and abdomen.

▪ Pull in your stomach and tighten it and your entire abdomen as much as you can. Build up this tension, and study it . . . Now relax and feel all the tension leaving these muscles . . . Note how relaxed and loose they are . . . Relax more and more . . .

▪ Once again, pull in your stomach and tighten your abdomen. Build up this tension, study it . . . Now release the tension and note the change . . . Pull in your stomach once more and tighten your abdomen as much as you can. Study this tension for a few moments . . . Now relax. Release all of the tension in your stomach and abdominal muscles . . . Continue relaxing for a few moments . . .

▪ Next, inhale deeply, push your diaphragm down, extend your stomach, and tense your abdomen as tight as you can. Study this tension . . . Now exhale and relax all the muscles in your stomach and abdomen . . . Enjoy this feeling for a few moments . . .

▪ Once more, inhale deeply, push your diaphragm down, extend your stomach, and tense your abdomen as tight as you can. Study this tension . . . Now exhale and relax, releasing all the tension from that area . . . Enjoy the feeling of decreasing tension . . . Continue breathing in and out for a while. Concentrate on relaxing more and more . . . Let all the tension out of the muscles in your abdomen, as well as in the rest of your body . . . As your muscles become more and more relaxed, you feel warm and somewhat sleepy . . .

I'm sorry he can't come to the phone right now . . . he's practicing his muscle re-laxation exercises!

RELAXING YOUR LOWER BACK, HIPS, THIGHS, AND CALVES

These exercises will last four to six minutes. As you relax more and more, concentrate next on your lower back.

- First, arch your lower back, and tense the muscles there as tight as you can. Build up the tension, study it . . . Now relax and note the change . . . Think about relaxing your lower back as much as you can . . . Relax your entire body more and more . . . deeper and deeper . . .
- Once again, arch up your lower back and tense the muscles there as tight as you can. Study this tension for a few moments . . . Now relax and notice the difference . . .

- Next, tense the muscles in your buttocks, thighs, hips, legs, and calves by flexing your buttocks as tight as you can while you press down on the heels of your feet. Exert as much pressure as you can . . . Build up this tension . . . study it . . . Now relax and note the change . . . Concentrate on relaxing all of your muscles, deeper and deeper . . .
- Once again, flex your buttocks and press down hard on your heels, build up the tension . . . study it . . . Now, relax and notice the change . . . Enjoy this feeling for a few moments . . .

- Next, while resting the heels of your feet, point your toes toward your head and tense all the muscles in your feet, ankles, and lower legs. Build up this tension . . . study it . . . Now relax and once more note the difference. Notice how good you feel . . .
- Once more, point your toes toward your head, and tense all of the muscles in your feet, ankles, and lower legs, build up this tension. Study it . . . Now relax and note the change . . . Notice how soothing it is to relax . . . Let the feeling spread through your body. Enjoy relaxing for a while . . .

FINAL INSTRUCTIONS

Continue to rest and relax as you go through the final set of instructions. These instructions should enhance and intensify the general overall state of deep muscle relaxation you've achieved already. They'll last about two to six minutes.

By now all your muscles should be fairly well relaxed. Your arms feel heavy, and you feel a warm sensation in all parts of your body.

- Now, add to your relaxation by taking a deep breath again. Fill your lungs completely, and hold this tension for a few moments . . . Then relax and exhale slowly . . . Notice how relaxed you feel as you exhale . . . Breathe normally for a while, and concentrate on relaxing more deeply . . .

- Once again, breathe in deeply, fill your lungs as full as you can, and hold your breath for a few moments . . . Study the tension . . . Now, exhale slowly and notice the increased relaxation as you do . . . Breathe normally for a while, and think about getting rid of all the tension in your body . . . You'll become more and more relaxed as you breathe in and out . . . The relaxation will go deeper and deeper . . .

- Now, once again breathe in deeply and fill your lungs as full as you can . . . Hold your breath for a few moments and study the tension . . . Now relax and notice how much more relaxed you are . . . Continue breathing normally for a while and, as you do, you become even more and more relaxed . . . deeper and deeper . . . You should now be completely relaxed . . . Enjoy this state . . . Enjoy the very warm, rewarding feeling of complete relaxation . . .

chapter 6

instructions for self-directed systematic desensitization

You've read the principles systematic desensitization is based on, and roughly what it involves. You've made up your hierarchy, and learned the tricks of relaxing deeply. Now you should be ready to begin the actual desensitization part of the program. Begin by planning how often you'll apply the program. We suggest at least twice a week. You should also arrange to meet with your behavior therapist once in a while. He or she will help you work through any problems you may have with your program, and assess your progress.

You'll find a checklist (see Appendix 2) that will help you keep track of your progress through the program. It lists the various tasks in the technique; such as, building the hierarchy, mastering the exercises, and so on. The form also has space for you to record what goes on during each session; such as, the number of times you imagine each scene, how many suds you feel, etc. It's quite important to track your progress on this form as you go. Not only will it help you see where you've been and where you're going, but it will also let your therapist look at your progress.

Read the following instructions fully. Make sure you understand them *before* you try your first session. Discuss any problems that aren't covered, with your therapist.

PREPARING

Arrange to be in a quiet room where no one will bother you when you prepare for each session. You may have to kick out your roommates, lover(s), kids, spouse, even your pets, for a while, but any noise will disrupt your relaxing and make it harder for you to imagine the scenes. Have either a tape-recorded or written version of the exercises near at hand. Put your deck of hierarchy cards in order with the first scene being the one with the lowest suds score. Have your checklist handy so you can record the results of your session as you finish.

Then, sit down in an easy chair or lounge. (A Freudian-type couch is acceptable, but not required.) Then get as comfortable as you can, and begin the following steps.

STEPS IN DESENSITIZATION

Step One: Relax Fully

Get completely relaxed. Take as long as you need to do this. After a while, you'll be able to relax in just a few minutes, though at first it may take longer. *Don't* go on to the next step until you're *fully* relaxed. Just think about relaxing deeply, and enjoy.

Step Two: Visualize the Hierarchy Scene

Once you're completely relaxed, turn to your first card — the one with the lowest suds level. Remaining as relaxed as you can, imagine the scene as clearly as possible for about ten seconds. Concentrate on relaxing completely as you imagine the scene. After ten seconds, stop visualizing.

If you felt *no anxiety* when you visualized (less than five suds), you're ready for the next scene. But before you pick up the next card, relax for about two minutes. Then, repeat step two with this next card.

If you felt more than five suds of anxiety, go to step three.

Step Three: Regain Relaxation, and Reimagine the Scene

(Use this step only if you felt more than five suds of anxiety.) Turn your card face down, and relax deeply. Relax for two or three minutes, or however long it takes to gain a fully relaxed state. Now, pick up the scene again and imagine it for ten seconds more. Concentrate on remaining relaxed the whole time you're doing this. Then stop the scene. If you still felt more than five suds of anxiety, repeat this step once again. If you felt no discomfort, relax for a moment and move on to the next scene, going back to step two.

Do this with each card in your hierarchy. Notice that you never go on to the next scene until you can visualize the one before without anxiety. And don't rush, or worry if you don't feel you're going fast enough. Take your time. You may have to imagine a certain scene a number of times before you're able to relax properly. But, sooner or later you'll be able to visualize high suds scenes without feeling anxious. At this point, you'll be ready to go on to the next card.

Step Four: Keep Track of Your Progress

At the end of your session, complete your checklist. Record the scenes you visualized, the number of times you did, and the suds levels you experienced.

SOME HINTS AND GUIDELINES

The following are a few hints to use as general guidelines. Read them carefully, and make sure you understand them.

1. Relax for 20 minutes before each session. You can reduce this later to whatever length of time you need, but make sure you're totally relaxed before you begin visualizing. *This is very important.*
2. Begin each new session by thinking about the last hierarchy scene that didn't cause anxiety in the last session. If you feel discomfort, go back to the previous scenes, until you reach one where you don't feel anxious. Then, go on from there.
3. After each scene, don't think of anything but relaxing. Do this for about two minutes before going on.
4. You should imagine each scene at least twice, even if the scene doesn't cause anxiety on the first try.
5. If you find that you can't completely relax during a session, stop. Try it again later, when conditions are better.
6. Plan for your session to last 20 to 30 minutes past the time you need to become initially relaxed. Don't be upset if you can only view one or two scenes a session without getting tense. Each person has their own rate. Some move quickly at the beginning of the hierarchy, and slow down at the end. It may be the other way around for others. In any case, remember to take your time. Enjoy what you're doing and the results your efforts promise.
7. If you do have a scene which causes major problems, you may be trying to go too fast. You might have too large a suds difference

between that scene and the one before it. If so, design a new item whose suds value falls between the two, and try that one first.

8. Talk over any problems that aren't dealt with here, with your therapist. Chances are, he or she has a fair amount of experience with this technique, and can see problems that you can't.

ONCE YOUR HIERARCHY IS FINISHED

After you go all the way through your list without feeling any anxiety, try to expose yourself gradually to real-life conditions relating to your previous fear. But don't jump in all at once. Start with brief periods of time first; and, as you begin to feel more sure of yourself, try it for longer periods of time, until there are no uneasy feelings left. You'll find the more you face these things, the more relaxed you'll become.

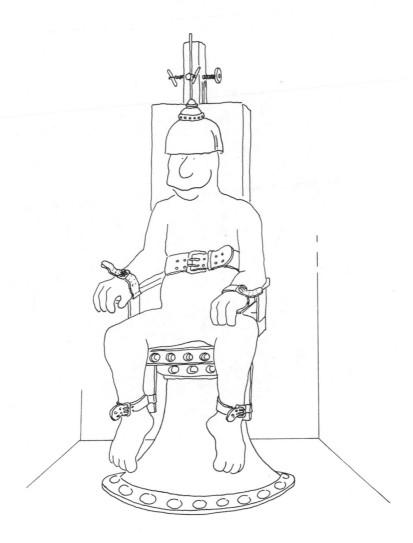

And to think . . . I used to be afraid of electrical appliances!

Honestly Harold, I don't know why you're getting so upset about a silly little spider!

section 3

systematic desensitization

its history, variations & problems

chapter 7
the history of systematic desensitization

In the first part of this manual we outlined the concepts and steps you'll need to apply systematic desensitization to yourself. We'll look at its history, variations, and potential problems in the sections that follow. We don't mean to give you an endless review of the ever-growing mountain of research on this technique. Many good books already do this. We've included several in the "suggested readings" list in Appendix 3. But, we do hope to give you a working knowledge of the technique and its problems, in an informal but concise way; and to provide references to the research literature, thus encouraging you to explore it further if you wish to. Without further ado, then, let's take a look at where it all began.

BEGINNINGS

On December 16th, 1941, Andrew Salter, a psychologist, sat in his office across from a surgeon who had a fear of enclosed spaces, a fear he'd lived with since he was seven or eight years old. They were meeting for the first time. By their sixth meeting, the surgeon's fear was gone, leaving in its wake a calm, amazed ex-claustrophobic.

Salter had managed this striking "cure" through a technique much like today's systematic desensitization. He told the surgeon to imagine fearful scenes while remaining relaxed. Instead of deep muscle relaxation, however, the client used hypnotic "self-suggestion" to put himself into a relaxed state. (Salter, 1949). This was the first report of applying a desensitization-like technique to the problem of learned fear.

At the same time, Joseph Wolpe was doing research with cats — work destined to become the springboard for the later growth of systematic desensitization. He delivered electric current to cats through

chapter 8
variations of systematic desensitization

Wolpe presented his techniques in 1958 in *Psychotherapy by Recip-rocal Inhibition.* Since then, therapists from a variety of backgrounds and theoretical camps have widely used the technique; and it has be-come a "household word" in therapy circles. It has grown and ex-panded, adapted and transformed, in recent years, taking on as many forms and faces as the many and varied people who've adopted it and made it work. Let's take a look at some of these variations, and what researchers have done with them, beginning with Wolpe's original concept.

INDIVIDUAL-TRADITIONAL

The most common type of systematic desensitization is a one-to-one client-therapist relationship. The client plays a passive role, the therapist guiding him or her through the phases of the program, de-signing the hierarchies, training the client to relax, and presenting the scenes. Of course, therapists differ widely in how they do this. Some spend more time training their people to relax and designing hierar-chies, than others. Some combine hypnosis with relaxing. And some prefer to use a specific type of hierarchy (such as a theme-oriented one), while others use several kinds, combining the sorts of items they feel are required by the specific fear they're working with. But research shows that even fairly wide variation can be used in the basic one-to-one plan, without losing its effect in getting rid of learned fears.

MASSED SESSIONS

In the standard type of desensitization, the therapist sees the client for an hour, once or twice a week, the process taking several weeks to complete. But recently, some therapists have tried holding several sessions over a short span of time, seeing the client for one to three hours several times a week, and ending up within a couple of weeks. This grouping of sessions over a short period of time is called **massed sessions.**

Robinson and Suinn (1969) described one of the first successful uses of this technique. They saw 20 spider phobics for five one-hour sessions, five days in a row. The result? All of their clients reported decreased anxiety related to spiders.

Dawley and Wenrich (1973) carried out massed sessions in a similar way, working with nursing students afraid of taking exams. They met with one group of nurses for three, two-hour and twenty-minute desensitization sessions over an eight-day period. Another group with the same fear, listened to lectures on good study habits, concentration, and learning, for the same amount of time, while a third group received no treatment at all. The massed session desensitization technique turned out to be the best, its group showing more fear-reduction than either of the other two.

Massed sessions have several benefits over weekly or twice-weekly ones. For one thing, they're often more suited to the therapist and client, being especially useful where clients need immediate help with their problems. This approach is also quicker, reducing the need to repeat instructions and hierarchy scenes, compared to meetings held less often.

IN-VIVO SYSTEMATIC DESENSITIZATION

In-vivo desensitization begins the same way as the standard approach: the client has learned to relax, and helps to make a hierarchy. But, instead of the client imagining the scenes, the therapist presents *actual* fear stimuli, beginning with those that produce little or no anxiety, and slowly moving to scenes causing the most fear.

Take a person with an intense fear of cats, for instance. He or she might first view a cat from 50 feet away, while deeply relaxed, trying to remain as calm as possible. Slowly, the distance is reduced to 45 feet, 40 feet, and so on, until the client can even pet the furry creature without fear.

As you can see, the in-vivo method is a good technique for people who have a hard time imagining scenes from their hierarchy. It also

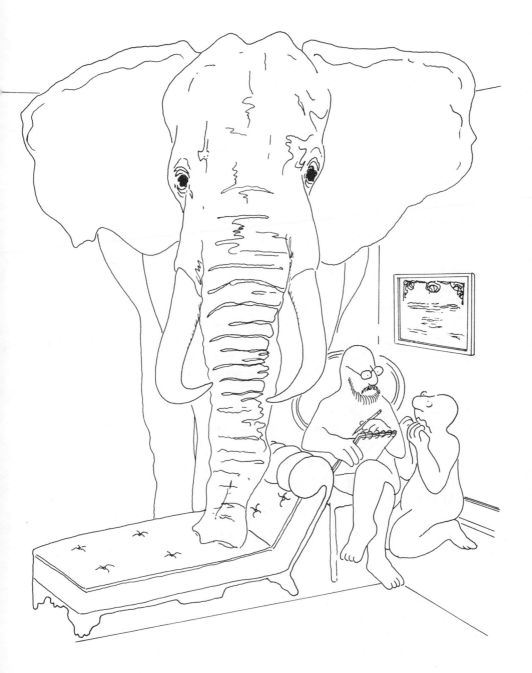

*At least **try** to imagine it 45 feet away!*

works along with other types of desensitization, like massed sessions. The in-vivo technique is sometimes a bit more time-consuming than the standard approach, practically speaking. It often requires going out and digging up the fear stimuli. (It can also get a little costly, as in the case of a fear of trans-Atlantic flights, long ocean voyages, or elephants.)

IN-VITRO SYSTEMATIC DESENSITIZATION

Related to the in-vivo technique, in-vitro desensitization involves presenting fear stimuli through media like pictures, slides, films, recordings, and videotape. The basic technique remains the same, as with in-vivo, differing only in the way the hierarchy scenes are presented. The client actually sees and hears the sights and sounds coupled with the feared event, while staying relaxed and safe away from the real threats or dangers.

Woody and Schauble (1969) use the catchy title, "Videotaped Vicarious Desensitization", in describing one variation of this technique. Their in-vitro hierarchy shows a series of videotaped scenes with a model getting closer and closer to a live snake.

Using a similar plan, Fryrear and Warner (1970) used a videotaped modeling technique for a nursing student's fear of dissecting animals. This woman was soon able to cut up with the best of them, after viewing scenes of a model doing more and more advanced dissecting with many kinds of animals.

As you can see, the therapist could easily change this approach to a self-directed technique, simply by having the clients work the equipment themselves.

GROUP SYSTEMATIC DESENSITIZATION

Two's company, three's a crowd. Or a group, depending on how you look at it. Arnold Lazarus (1961) was the first therapist to report using desensitization in a group setting. And many other studies have affirmed the value of dealing with learned fears in this way, since his initial research.

Again, the techniques share the same basis as the standard approach. Only now, more people are involved. You can design hierarchy items for each member, or use one standard sequence of scenes for the whole group. The total time you need for group desensitization is usually a little more than the average for one-client sessions, the rate of the group's progress being determined, of course, by the slowest member. But, the savings in therapist time is clearly large, making this technique quite thrifty, and comfortably available to many people with learned fears.

AUTOMATED SYSTEMATIC DESENSITIZATION

Since the time systematic desensitization was first introduced, many people have tried to standardize its steps. The result? Recorded exercises for deep muscle relaxation, and automatic presentations of hierarchy scenes.

The first person to design a fully automatic "desensitizor" was Peter Lang, in 1969. He called his device DAD — Device for Automated Desensitization. DAD was really a computer, a mechanical therapist programmed to carry out the many stages of desensitization. But instead of greyish ooze, DAD's brain was made up of taped exercises, hierarchies, and instructions. DAD followed the usual process, telling its clients to "stop imagining and relax again", when they reported anxiety during a scene. And, it wouldn't give the next scene until the previous item could be imagined without fear. DAD did a pretty good job, and Lang concluded that automatic desensitization may be as effective as that given by real, flesh-and-blood therapists.

Since DAD's debut, others have tried this also, getting similar results. Donner and Guerney (1969) used an automated group desensitization program for test anxiety. Actually, they tried to find out whether the presence of a human therapist was important or not. So, an actual therapist was used with one group of people, while another group was desensitized by a tape-recorded program. Both worked, resulting in better grades for the two groups, along with reports of less anxiety when taking tests.

Colter (1970) has also reported success with an automated program for fear of snakes. His "therapist" was actually a modified dictating machine with a series of tapes on relaxation training, visualization, and scene presentation.

Researchers' results with this approach look fairly good, suggesting that desensitization can be done with a machine nearly as well as it can with a real therapist. And the automated techniques pay off, in terms of saving the therapist time (not to mention the client, money).

But problems do exist. Paul and Trimble (1970) have pointed out that automatic therapists may not be as sensitive to the fact that different clients learn things at different speeds, for instance in in vivo desensitization of the client's fears (Donner, 1970). You can see this could be pretty useful where social fears are involved, the therapist acting as a mild fear stimulus during the process. Donner also suggests that a live therapist can motivate and help a client better than a machine, making it more likely that the client will follow through with all steps of the plan. Indeed, you'd be less likely to fall asleep or avoid imagining fearful scenes if a therapist were there instead of a machine.

All these problems point to at least one caution, one most therapists are familiar with: frequent checks of client progress are important to therapeutic success. And this is true no matter what kind of program you use. This is also why we've suggested using this manual with the help of a behavior therapist.

SELF-DIRECTED SYSTEMATIC DESENSITIZATION

By now, you're all familiar with this variation of the basic plan. Self-directed desensitization can be a lot like the automatic techniques we talked about in the last section. But it differs in one important way. Here, the client controls the show, setting his or her own pace through the program.

Minger and Wolpe (1967) were the first therapists to give this a try, using a client with a fear of public speaking. After he learned to relax, the therapists automated the sessions so the client could hold them at home. His "do-it-yourself" kit had pre-recorded exercises, followed by instructions for imagining the various scenes from his hierarchy. After only seven sessions, the client had "cured" himself, and was able to speak in public again. Checking up on him eight months later, the therapists found him still able to talk in front of an audience with ease.

Kahn and Baker (1968) compared the effects of therapist- versus self-conducted programs with students having a variety of learned fears. They divided the students into two groups — one coming in for desensitization from a therapist, the other working at home with a do-it-yourself kit. Their kit had a manual of instructions (Kahn and Sandler, 1966), along with a record of exercises. The do-it-yourselfers were called weekly by the therapist for a progress check, although they carried out the steps pretty much on their own. Within six weeks, both groups had reduced their learned fears equally, suggesting that having a therapist give the technique may not work any better than giving it yourself. But, the clients weren't entirely on their own, even in the self-administered group. They talked to the therapist once a week over the phone.

Taking this one step further, Phillips, Johnson, and Geyer (1972) compared completely self-conducted desensitization with a therapist-assisted program. The technique in the two groups was about the same, both having a do-it-yourself kit. But, in the therapist-assisted group, the clients got help in putting their lists together and learning to relax. In this study, it turned out that completely self-administered desensitization may be a little less powerful than a therapist-assisted plan.

Self-directed desensitization has also worked with patients on a psychiatric ward. One patient designed his own program for reducing a fear of walking in crowds, using a manual and taped exercises. His fear of walking in crowds had disappeared after four weeks of the program. And the change lasted. When researchers checked back nine months later no problem existed (Dawley, Guidry, and Curtis, 1973).

Hopefully, with manuals such as the one you're reading becoming available, we'll be seeing more and more of this kind of research with different types of fears, and different kinds of people; but according to the research we have thus far, it certainly seems to work. Self-directed desensitization appears to be a viable option to the more costly and time-consuming kinds of traditional, therapist-administered programs.

chapter 9
problems in systematic desensitization

We've seen that systematic desensitization is a very good way of handling learned anxiety and related behavioral problems. But it's not perfect, nor all powerful. It's limited, like anything else. It isn't always the best procedure to use — at least not by itself — people, problems, and situations differ. A behavior therapist with experience can best judge the ideal. We've suggested that you use this manual under the guidance of such a person for this very reason. However, there are situations where systematic desensitization may not be the best technique to use in dealing with the problem. We'd like to point out a few of these.

THE PROBLEM OF SECONDARY GAIN

A person may not want to give up a problem if it results in a fair amount of reward, "sympathy", or if it removes responsibility. As strange as it sounds, discomfort often becomes an asset, helping someone to avoid work, escape from unpleasant scenes, or get "pity" and attention they don't otherwise get. And, they would, sometimes, rather remain fearful than return to their once "normal" existence. We call these types of rewards **secondary gains**.

Think of a pilot who develops a fear of flying, which isn't as far-fetched as it may seem. If it were strong enough, the anxiety could keep the pilot grounded, unable to carry out his or her job. This may not be as bad as you might think, if the job were a drag and boring in the first place. Add a touch of well-timed sympathy to this, and you're dealing with a more complex situation.

In cases like this "symptom-substitution" may occur. Symptom substitution describes the situation where one problem behavior is done away with but another crops up in its place — a problem supposedly stemming from some underlying source. This notion is based on the medical-model approach to behavior problems, which says that problem behaviors are merely "symptoms" of an underlying "mental illness". According to this view, if all you do is remove the behavior (symptom), but fail to deal with the underlying conflict (illness), another problem will take its place sooner or later. In other words, once we successfully reduce phobic anxiety, we might expect something else to replace it; a relapse, perhaps, or another behavior problem, such as stuttering, a muscle tic, or nightmares.

We may indeed find a return of the phobia, or another behavior problem, if a great deal of secondary gain is present. Not because we've failed to cure the disease, but because we've removed a large source of **reward**. In these situations, it's a good practice to train other acts that produce rewards — ones more fitting, more in line with success in life — to thwart further problem behaviors that might develop.

This isn't much of a problem in most phobias, luckily. People with learned fears often feel like victims, helpless to control their overwhelming arousal. But once the learned fear is unlearned, the person adjusts to his or her behavior with a new sense of freedom, no longer having to avoid or fear things that are harmless, in reality.

You see, the old adage, "you can only change if you want to", holds some truth. The prospect for change may well be low where motivation is poor, secondary gains high, and the chance to escape from responsibilities at hand. Other methods will have to be combined with the desensitization approach in cases like these.

FREE-FLOATING ANXIETY

The technique of systematic desensitization was designed to deal mainly with anxiety focused around a particular object or theme — fear — which, in a sense, is "bound" to some stimulus situation. We need other techniques to handle pervading anxiety, anxiety that occurs regardless of what's going on in the environment. Although desensitization may well be included in the change program for such "free-floating anxiety", by itself it's a poor choice.

INABILITY TO EXPERIENCE DECREASES IN ANXIETY DURING RELAXATION

Most people quickly learn deep muscle relaxation from exercises like those we've looked at. And, they experience a marked decrease in anxiety once they relax. But, there are some individuals who don't. Some people just can't relax enough to squelch their feelings of fear. In these cases, the basic technique may still be used, but with other options, such as drugs, hypnosis, the use of anger, or sexual arousal.

PROBLEMS IN VISUALIZING

Desensitization is based on the idea that a person reacts to imagined scenes in much the same way they would react in an actual phobic state. As we said earlier, this requires vivid and clear imagination, putting the person right into the scene, making them interact with the stimuli, feeling all the arousal sensations that they would feel if such a scene really happened. In other words, imagining phobic scenes while unrelaxed should result in fairly intense arousal. But, in some, this doesn't occur, due to poor visualization.

Problems in visualization can be handled by using "live" phobic stimuli (in-vivo), or other techniques including slides, records, or videotapes (in-vitro). For further explanations of these themes, you might review the sections on in-vivo and in-vitro desensitization.

RESISTING THE METHOD

This problem is quite similar to the first one we discussed above, and usually stems from the same sources. There are people who feel this type of procedure is "shallow" or "machine-like", taking the point of view that it doesn't really get to the "roots" of their anxiety. They tend to ignore the evidence that it's really a very effective method, and has a high success rate in a large percentage of phobic cases. As we've seen, follow-ups done in these studies find little or no return of the problem, for the most part, suggesting that if the roots haven't been dealt with in an adequate way, they've shrunken and died on their own, anyway.

But some people insist on this position. In these cases the person will probably not carry out the program consistently. The program won't succeed as well as it might have under better conditions, as a result.

CONCLUSIONS

So, we've looked at the theory of systematic desensitization, its strengths and weaknesses, some of its variations, and their roots in the research works. But what does it all mean?

It means this: Systematic desensitization is a fairly direct, rapid way of reducing learned fears, whether a therapist, a machine, or you administer it. It's a technique that allows you a lot of leeway in program design, giving you room for problems like time limits, the need for quick relief from anxiety, varied and sometimes unusual types of learned fear stimuli, and trouble in relaxing and visualizing. The various forms of desensitization we've looked at can be combined or changed to custom-fit nearly any kind of phobic problem, in nearly any kind of setting.

Self-directed programs are distinctly promising and exciting. They provide a way for almost anyone who wants to change, to reduce their learned fears, successfully and economically, with only brief contacts with a therapist. They also make the technique available to many people who couldn't otherwise afford it, or who find it hard to take time off for frequent visits to the hospital or clinic.

But, perhaps one of the most important aspects of self-directed desensitization relates to **self-control,** and the positive feeling of fulfillment that comes with solving your own problems. The person who actively carries out a plan toward making their lot in life better and more rewarding is bound to feel better about themself. They're also likely to feel more confident and "in control" when dealing with other problems, or in overcoming the many and varied challenges that confront us daily, prodding us along the many paths toward our goals.

And that, as the saying goes, ain't all bad.

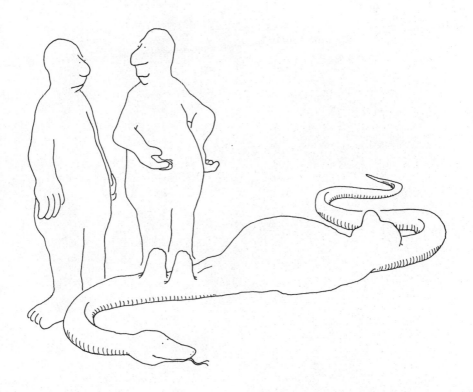

At least he proved he's no longer afraid of snakes!

references

Cotler, S. B. Sex differences and generalization of anxiety reduction with automated desensitization and minimal therapist interaction. *Behaviour Research and Therapy*, 1970, 8, 273-285.

Dawley, H. H., Guidry, L. S., & Curtis, E. Self-administered desensitization on a psychiatric ward: A case report. *Journal of Behavior Therapy and Experimental Psychiatry*, 1973, 4, 301-303.

Dawley, H. H., & Wenrich, W. W. *Patient's manual for systematic desensitization.* Veterans Workshop, Veterans Administration Hospital, Palo Alto, Calif., 1973.

Dawley, H. H., & Wenrich, W. W. Massed group desensitization in the reduction of test anxiety. *Psychological Reports*, 1973, 33, 359-363.

Donner, L. Automated group desensitization: A follow-up report. *Behaviour Research and Therapy*, 1970, 8, 241-247.

Donner, L., & Gurney, B. G. Automated group desensitization for test anxiety. *Behaviour Research and Therapy*, 1969, 7, 1-13.

Fryrear, J. L., & Werner, S. Treatment of a phobia by use of a video-taped modeling procedure: A case study. *Behavior Therapy*, 1970, 1, 391-394.

Jacobson, E. *Progressive relaxation.* Chicago: University of Chicago Press, 1938.

Johnson, S. M. *The effects of desensitization and relaxation on the treatment of test anxiety.* Unpublished master's thesis, Northwestern University, 1966.

Kahn, M., & Baker, B. Desensitization with minimal therapist contact. *Journal of Abnormal Psychology*, 1968, 73, 198-200.

Kahn, M., & Sandler, A. *A manual for systematic desensitization.* Unpublished manuscript, 1966.

Lang, P. J. The on-line computer in behavior therapy research. *American Psychologist*, 1969, 24, 236-239.

Lazarus, A. A. Group therapy of phobic disorders by systematic desensitization. *Journal of Abnormal and Social Psychology*, 1961, 63, 504-510.

Mingler, B., & Wolpe, J. Automated self-desensitization: A case report. *Behaviour Research and Therapy*, 1967, 5, 133-135.

Paul, G. L., & Trimble, R. W. Recorded vs. "live" relaxation training and hypnotic suggestion: Comparative effectiveness for reducing physiological arousal and inhibiting stress response. *Behavior Therapy*, 1970, 1, 285-302.

Phillips, R. E., Johnson, G. D., & Gayer, A. Self-administered systematic desensitization. *Behaviour Research and Therapy*, 1972, 10, 93-96.

Robinson, C., & Suinn, R. M. Group desensitization of a phobia in a massed session. *Behaviour Research and Therapy*, 1969, 7, 319-321.

Salter, A. *Conditioned reflex therapy: The direct approach to the reconstruction of personality*. New York: Creative Age Press, 1961.

Suinn, R. M., & Hall, R. Marathon desensitization groups: An innovative technique. *Behaviour Research and Therapy*, 1970, 8, 97-98.

Wolpe, J. Experimental neurosis as learned behavior. *British Journal of Psychology*, 1952, 43, 243-268.

Wolpe, J. *Psychotherapy by reciprocal inhibition*. Stanford: Stanford University Press, 1958.

Wolpe, J. *The practice of behavior therapy* (2nd ed.). New York: Pergamon Press, 1973.

Wolpe, J., & Lazarus, A. A. *Behavior therapy techniques: A guide to the treatment of neuroses*. New York: Pergamon Press, 1966.

Woody, R., & Schauble, P. G. Videotaped vicarious desensitization. *Journal of Nervous and Mental Disease*, 1969, 148, 281-286.

appendix 1
sample anxiety-stimulus hierarchies

FEAR OF CATS

1. You're sitting in a comfortable chair in the safety of your home watching TV.
2. You're watching a commercial for cat food — no cat is visible.
3. The commercial continues and a cat is now eating the food.
4. A man is now petting the cat.
5. A man is holding the cat and fondling it.
6. A woman is holding the cat, and the cat is licking her hands and face.
7. You're looking out the window of your home and you see a cat on the lawn across the street.
8. You're sitting in front of your house, and you see a cat walk by on the sidewalk across the street.
9. You're sitting in your yard, and you see a cat walk by on your sidewalk.
10. A cat walks within 15 feet of you.
11. A friend of yours picks the cat up and plays with it.
12. Your friend is ten feet away from you, and the cat is licking his face.
13. Your friend comes within five feet of you while he's holding the cat.
14. Your friend stands two feet away and plays with the cat.
15. Your friend asks you if you'd like to pet the cat.
16. Your friend reaches out and offers you the cat.
17. He puts the cat on the ground, and it walks over to you.
18. The cat rubs up against your leg.
19. The cat walks between your legs purring.
20. You reach down and touch the cat.
21. You pet the cat.
22. You pick the cat up and pet it.

FEAR OF RIDING IN A CROWDED ELEVATOR
(Maximum capacity — 12 people)

1. You're walking into a building which has an elevator.
2. You're walking down the hall toward the elevator.
3. You're standing alone in front of the elevator.
4. One person joins you in front of the elevator.
5. The doors open, and you and the other person enter the empty elevator.
6. The elevator goes to the second floor, and one other person enters.
7. It goes to the third floor, and another person enters.
8. It goes to the next floor, and one more person enters.
9. It goes a floor higher, and another person enters (a total of six people).
10. It goes to the next floor, and the seventh person enters (beginning to get crowded).
11. It goes to the next floor, and the eighth person enters (more crowded).
12. It goes to the next floor, and the ninth person enters.
13. It goes to the next floor, and the tenth person enters (fairly full).
14. It goes to the next floor, and the eleventh person enters (crowded).
15. It goes to the next floor, and the twelfth person enters (packed full).

FEAR OF CROWDS

1. You're leaving home and heading downtown for a shopping trip.
2. You're walking along a street, and see a large number of people waiting for a bus on the other side of the street.
3. You're driving in a car, and pass a large crowd of people on the street.
4. You're standing at a bus stop with your husband.
5. You're standing next to one person at a bus stop when two others come and join you.
6. You're standing at a bus stop with five other people.
7. You're standing at a bus stop with seven other people.
8. You're standing at a bus stop with ten other people.
9. You're standing at a bus stop with 15 other people.
10. You're in the center of a group of seven people.
11. You're approaching the fringe of a moderate-sized crowd of ten people.
12. You're on the fringe of a moderate-sized crowd of 15 noisy people.
13. You're almost in the middle of a moderate-sized crowd of 15 noisy people.
14. You're in the middle of a moderate-sized crowd of 15 noisy people.
15. You're approaching the fringe of a large crowd of 35 noisy people.
16. You're on the fringe of a large crowd of 35 jostling, noisy people.
17. You're almost in the middle of a large, jostling crowd of 35 noisy people.
18. You're standing in the midst of a large, jostling crowd of 35 noisy people.

FEAR OF DARKNESS

1. You're walking down a well-lit street at night, only a few shadows here and there.

2. You're walking through a park at night with large lights placed every 50 yards along the path. In between lights many trees and bushes cast long shadows.

3. You're in your bedroom at home, with only a small lamp across the room.

4. You're entering your living room which is lighted by only two candles.

5. You're entering your bedroom lighted by a small night light only. You can still see all the furniture in the room.

6. You're walking down a street where the lights are 100 yards apart. For a short time it's almost completely dark between lights.

7. You're lying in bed with the room lit only by the moonlight coming through the window. You can still make out the shapes of the furniture.

8. You're walking down an unlighted street with only a flashlight to find your way.

9. You're entering your bedroom which is very dimly lit by starlight. You see dark shapes which you know are furniture by their locations.

10. You're walking down a street with lights spaced every 200 yards. You are in darkness for about 20 seconds between lights.

11. You're entering your bedroom which is in total darkness. You can find the furniture only by its location in the room.

12. You're walking along an unlighted street. You can only see about 20 feet in front of you.

13. You're lying in bed with the lights on when suddenly the power goes off. You stumble around the house in total darkness looking for candles.

14. You're walking along a street in complete darkness. You lose your way several times but make it home finally.

FEAR OF EATING IN CROWDED RESTAURANTS

1. You're walking down the street on a bright, cheerful day.

2. You're looking in the window of a restaurant with a few people in it.

3. You're getting ready to enter a restaurant with a few people in it.

4. You're walking into a restaurant with a few people in it.

5. You're sitting on the left side of a restaurant with a few people in it with your back to them.

6. You're sitting on the left side of a restaurant, facing a few people.

7. You're eating in the center of a restaurant with a few people in it.

8. You're walking by a restaurant that's one-third full, looking in, and seeing people staring at you.

9. You're walking by a restaurant that's half full, looking in, and seeing people staring at you.

10. You're walking by the inside entrance to a crowded restaurant, looking in, and seeing people staring at you.

11. You're sitting in a restaurant that's one-third full, with your back to the other people.

12. You're sitting on the left side of a restaurant that's one-third full, with people staring at you.

13. You're sitting in the center of a restaurant that's one-third full, with people staring at you.

14. You're sitting at a crowded table in the middle of a half-full restaurant with everyone staring at you.

15. You're sitting at a side table in a crowded restaurant with people staring at you.

16. You're eating at a crowded table in one corner of a crowded restaurant, facing everyone with everyone staring at you.

17. You're eating at a crowded table in the center of a noisy, crowded restaurant, with everyone staring at you.

TEST ANXIETY

1. You're going to be taking a series of I.Q. tests and course exams six months from now.
2. You're going to be taking a series of I.Q. tests and course exams three months from now.
3. It's two months before taking I.Q. tests and exams.
4. It's one month before taking I.Q. tests and exams.
5. It's three weeks before taking I.Q. tests and exams.
6. It's two weeks before taking I.Q. tests and exams.
7. It's one week before taking I.Q. tests and exams.
8. It's four days before taking I.Q. tests and exams.
9. It's three days before taking I.Q. tests and exams.
10. It's two days before taking I.Q. tests and exams.
11. You only have one day to go before taking I.Q. tests and exams.
12. It's the morning of tests.
13. It's three hours before tests and exams.
14. It's two hours before tests and exams.
15. It's one hour before tests and exams.
16. You only have thirty minutes to go before taking I.Q. tests and exams.
17. You're entering building where tests are to be given.
18. You're entering room where tests are to be given.
19. The examiner walks in room with tests.
20. The examiner passes out the tests and exams.
21. You're looking over and preparing to answer the questions.
22. You're answering the questions.
23. You find a question you can't answer.
24. After finding a question you can't handle, you go on, and then find another question you can't answer.
25. After several questions you can't answer, you complete the rest of the questions knowing that you're not doing too well.
26. You're turning in tests and exams with the sickening knowledge that you did very poorly.

FEAR OF AIRPLANE TRAVEL

1. You're at home thinking about taking a trip on an airplane.

2. You've scheduled an airplane trip, bought the tickets, and you're putting your luggage into your car and getting ready to go to the airport.

3. You're now driving to the airport and getting closer and closer.

4. You're parking your car at the airport and unloading the luggage.

5. You're at the ticket counter where the clerk is checking your tickets and your luggage.

6. You're in the airport lobby waiting for the number of your flight to be called on the public address system so you can board the plane.

7. You're boarding the plane and getting into a seat, fastening your safety belt.

8. The airplane has taxied and is now taking off and climbing to its cruising altitude.

9. The airplane has reached cruising altitude and is now flying to its destination. You can now loosen your seatbelt and walk about the plane. You may listen to music, eat or have cocktails or other refreshments.

10. You've been advised by the P.A. system that the plane is in its final glide path, and is about to descend and land. You land and the plane taxies to the unloading area and stops.

11. You get off the plane at the airport at your destination.

FEAR OF FIRE

1. You're watching a news story on TV about a house burning down.

2. You're standing 30 feet away watching a small bonfire.

3. You're striking a match and holding it as it burns down.

4. You're striking a match and lighting a gas burner under a pot on the stove.

5. You're holding a lighted candle as the wax melts and runs down the sides.

6. You're frying chicken on the stove, you splash some grease onto the burner and the flame flares up slightly.

7. You're standing ten feet away watching a small bonfire.

8. You're frying potatoes on the stove when the grease in the pan catches fire. You take out a can of flour and smother the flames.

9. You're standing five feet away from a small bonfire. You feel its warmth.

10. Someone drops a match into a waste basket. As it begins to flame up you take a bucket of water and douse the fire.

11. You're standing three feet away from a small bonfire. You feel your clothes and skin warming up on the side closest to the fire.

12. You're sitting in a theatre when you see a fire start about ten feet from you. You walk out calmly and tell the manager.

13. You're standing two feet away from a roaring bonfire. You hold your hands over the fire to warm them up.

14. You're walking into your bedroom, you see your bed engulfed in flames. You close the door and go to a neighbor's house to call the fire department.

15. You're walking down the street, you hear a fire truck coming. It stops 30 feet from you where a large house is engulfed in flames.

16. You're cooking a steak on the stove, you suddenly realize your apron has caught fire. You rip it off, throw it on the floor, and stomp out the flames.

FEAR OF DIRT

1. A small child comes into your house out of the rain and gets mud on your kitchen floor.

2. You're picking up the newspaper from the lawn, and get mud all over your hands.

3. You're washing the mud off your hands, and notice one spot just won't come off.

4. You're taking the dishes from the washer, and notice several are still dirty.

5. A young boy comes into your house shaking his clothes and sending up a cloud of dust all over the room.

6. As you start to eat supper, you notice some dirty spots on your plate.

7. You're eating at a restaurant, and notice the silverware and glasses are dirty.

8. Coming home after a dust storm, you see that a fine layer of dust has settled over everything in the house.

9. After cleaning the house, you look in the mirror to see dust in your hair, your clothes, and all over your body.

10. You're almost finished eating supper, when you see that your plate is filthy.

11. You're walking down the street in the rain, and a car passes by, splashing mud all over your shoes and legs, all the way up to your waist.

12. You're halfway through a coke, and notice trash floating in the bottom of the bottle.

13. As you eat, you taste something gritty and hard. Looking at your fork you see the remainder of a piece of dirt.

14. You're walking in the rain and a car passes, splashing you with mud from head to toe. You have mud in your hair, eyes, nose, and mouth.

FEAR OF SPIDERS

1. You see a large spider on the far wall of your room.
2. You see a large spider on the wall crawling toward you about six feet away.
3. A large spider crawls to about four feet away; to about two feet away.
4. You see a large spider dangling about two feet over your head.
5. You see a spider crawling toward you, one foot away.
6. You see a large spider dangling about one foot over your head.
7. You see ten large spiders crawling around your room.
8. You see a large spider crawling toward your hand, about two inches away.
9. You see a large spider crawling on your shoe, pant leg, shirt sleeve, bare foot, bare leg, bare arm, front of your shirt, shirt collar, your neck, on your face.
10. A large spider jumps at you.
11. A swarm of large spiders are crawling all over you.

FEAR OF ENCLOSED PLACES

1. You're sitting alone in a large room (20' x 20') with several doors and windows, some of them open.

2. You're walking around a large room and discover that all the doors and windows are closed.

3. You're waiting for a friend in a medium-sized room (12' x 14') and become aware that there are only one door and two small windows in the room.

4. You're walking down a long narrow hall and you notice there are no doors or windows on either side.

5. You enter a friend's study, she closes the door, and you realize that it's a small room (8' x 10') with no windows.

6. Your friend leaves the study, and you begin to wonder if she has locked the door.

7. You walk over to the door, and find that the door knob will not turn. After 10 seconds of fumbling you get the door to open.

8. You're unable to open the door and knock for 30 seconds before your friend returns to open the door.

9. You enter a walk-in closet and someone closes the door behind you by accident.

10. You turn toward the door, and see there's no door knob on the inside. You bang on the door for one minute before someone opens it.

11. You enter an elevator and stand there three minutes, doors open.

12. You're standing in the elevator, the doors close, and it starts to move up.

13. You're riding up in the elevator, and realize it's small with no windows.

14. The elevator stops at your floor, but the doors remain closed.

15. The elevator stops between floors. After five minutes it starts up again.

16. Walking into a small closet, you close the door and notice that there is hardly enough room to turn around.

FEAR OF HARMLESS SNAKES

1. You're in a museum looking at various species of stuffed snakes.
2. Walking across your yard, you see a small green garter snake ten feet away.
3. You're standing five feet away from a glass-enclosed king snake, two feet long.
4. You watch as someone reaches in and picks up the snake by the back of its neck.
5. As you watch, the snake begins to wind around the man's arm.
6. Sitting in a lawn chair, you look down and see a foot-long garter snake five feet away.
7. The man holds out the king snake four feet from you, and you see it flicking its tongue.
8. Walking across your yard, you see a green garter snake three feet away.
9. Holding the king snake firmly, the man takes two steps toward you (three feet away).
10. Walking up your driveway, you almost step on a small garter snake as it slithers out of the grass onto the pavement.
11. As the garter snake slides away, you reach down and touch its tail.
12. You reach down and grab the garter snake behind its head.
13. The man holds out the king snake, offering it to you.
14. You reach out and touch the leathery skin of the king snake.
15. Grabbing the king snake behind the head, you take it from the man.
16. Turning the snake's head toward you, you see it has a large mouth but no fangs.
17. The snake begins to wind around your arm.
18. The snake begins to hiss and flick its tongue at you.

FEAR OF SEXUAL INTERCOURSE
(Male)

1. Your partner invites you to her apartment.
2. At the apartment, she snuggles up and you embrace each other.
3. You begin to fondle your partner's breast.
4. Your partner caresses your genital area.
5. You expose one of your partner's breasts and begin to kiss it.
6. Your partner caresses your penis — through your clothing.
7. You massage your partner's vaginal area through her panties.
8. You pull her panties aside, and insert middle finger in vaginal area.
9. Your partner unzips your pants and exposes your penis.
10. You both caress each other.
11. Your partner undresses — you follow.
12. Nude, you both embrace again, and then move to the bedroom.
13. Your partner reclines on the bed and beckons to you.
14. You mount your partner, and slowly insert your penis into her vagina.
15. You thrust your penis in and out while on top of your partner.
16. You continue sexual intercourse to mutual climax.

FEAR OF SEXUAL INTERCOURSE
(Female)

1. During dinner, your partner brushes his knee against yours and smiles at you.
2. After dinner you and your partner sit on the sofa. He puts his arm around you.
3. Your partner leans over and kisses you.
4. Your partner pulls you to him and presses his body against yours.
5. Your partner caresses your breast through your blouse.
6. He unbuttons your blouse and exposes one of your breasts and kisses it.
7. He exposes both of your breasts and begins kissing them hard.
8. Your partner runs his hand up your thigh and caresses your vaginal area through your panties.
9. He pulls your panties aside, and inserts his finger in your vagina.
10. He pulls your panties down — and removes the rest of your clothing — and continues caressing you.
11. You both enter the bedroom — your partner undresses, and stands before you with an erection.
12. You clasp your hand around your partner's penis and massage it.
13. Your partner mounts you and inserts his penis.
14. Your partner thrusts his penis in and out while on top of you.
15. You continue sexual intercourse to mutual climax.

FEAR OF RECEIVING INJECTIONS

1. You're sitting at home in a comfortable chair watching TV as Dr. Welby gives a child a shot in the arm.

2. You're calling the doctor and making an appointment to go in and get a shot in two days.

3. You wake up and remember today's the day you have to go to get a shot.

4. You're driving to the doctor's office to get your shot.

5. You're sitting in the waiting room as a patient comes out holding her arm.

6. You go into the examining room and say hello to the doctor.

7. The nurse comes in to prepare the injection.

8. You watch the nurse as he inserts the needle into the bottle and draws the fluid into the syringe.

9. The nurse clears the air from the syringe, squirting a small amount of fluid into the air.

10. The nurse asks you to roll up your sleeve.

11. The nurse takes out a cotton ball and walks over to you.

12. The nurse wipes your arm with the cotton, and the alcohol cools your arm as it evaporates.

13. Out of the corner of your eye you see the needle moving toward your arm.

14. You feel a slight pinch as the needle enters your arm.

15. The nurse pushes the plunger on the syringe and you feel a mild burning sensation in your muscle.

16. The nurse removes the needle from your arm, and you see a small drop of blood from where the needle had been.

FEAR OF WEAPONS

1. You're at a museum looking at a display case full of antique guns.
2. You walk into your living room, and see a large hunting knife on a table 15 feet away.
3. You walk slowly over to the table.
4. You stand beside the table, and look at the long pointed blade of the knife.
5. You pick up the knife carefully, noticing how shiny and sharp the blade seems.
6. At a friend's home, he shows you his collection of rifles.
7. He takes one rifle out of the rack and walks toward you.
8. He holds out the rifle, offering it to you.
9. You reach out and take the rifle in both hands.
10. Your friend suddenly produces a revolver from a desk drawer.
11. The friend invites you down to his target range in the basement.
12. At the target range your friend points the gun at a target and fires. The blast echoes through the room.
13. Offering you the revolver, he asks you to take a shot at the target.
14. Taking the gun from him, you point it at the target and slowly squeeze the trigger.
15. As you squeeze the trigger, the gun fires, jerking your hand into the air.
16. Whittling a piece of wood with a sharp knife you cut your finger by accident.

FEAR OF AUTOMOBILES

1. You're walking up to a beautiful new car a friend has just bought.
2. You open the door of the car and see the plush carpet, padded dash, and well-stuffed bucket seats.
3. You sit down in the parked car with the door open, one foot on the ground.
4. You close the door and sink comfortably into the seat behind the steering wheel.
5. You shift the car into neutral, and it rolls forward about two feet.
6. With the brake on, you shift into park and turn the key, starting the motor.
7. You shift into drive, and drive down the driveway about 20 feet, slowly.
8. You shift into reverse, and back up the driveway about ten feet, slowly.
9. You back out of the driveway carefully, and drive around the block slowly.
10. You drive down to the local store (about four blocks) and return home.
11. You're driving over to a friend's home about two miles from your home.
12. You turn on to a street where several other cars are traveling.
13. You turn on to a busy street where several other cars are passing you on both sides.
14. You get on to the expressway and increase your speed to 55 MPH.
15. You're driving down a deserted street and a cat runs out in front of you.
16. You're driving in the rain, you start to skid but quickly regain control.
17. You're sitting at a stop light, and the car behind rolls up and bumps your car.
18. You turn a corner at five MPH, a car backs out and smashes into the side of your car.
19. You're driving down a two-lane road, the oncoming car swerves into your lane. You drive into the ditch to avoid hitting him.

FEAR OF BIRDS

1. Looking out the window, you see two or three small sparrows on the lawn.
2. As you watch, one sparrow flies up to light on a bush near the window.
3. Three or four more sparrows fly up to join the one on the bush.
4. One sparrow hops up on the window sill and looks at you.
5. Taking the trash out, you see two robins perched on the garbage can.
6. As you walk toward the birds they fly up and away, over your head.
7. Walking down the street you look up and see 10 or 15 robins perched on the telephone wires 30 feet above you.
8. As you continue walking, they take off in all directions fluttering their wings wildly.
9. Entering the park, you see about 25 pigeons walking around eating popcorn.
10. Passing a small tree, you see that it's filled with crows, cawing and flapping their wings.
11. You walk by a pond, and a small flock of ducks flies over your head and lands on the water.
12. As you sit on a bench, two or three pigeons walk around about eight feet away.
13. One pigeon walks up to within two feet of you to pick up some popcorn.
14. Holding some popcorn in your hand, you lean toward the pigeon.
15. The pigeon walks over and nibbles the popcorn from your hand.
16. As you walk home, a bluejay swoops down from a tree about ten feet away.
17. As you continue walking, the bluejay flies up and dives to within five feet of you.
18. Entering your living room, you discover that a robin has gotten in and is flying around the room. He/she flies within three feet of you.
19. You're walking down the street, and a large flock of geese fly over. The sky turns almost black with birds.

FEAR OF DEAD PEOPLE

1. Watching a funeral on TV, you see people carrying the casket into the church.
2. Arriving home, you learn a friend of the family has died.
3. You're driving down the street on your way to the funeral home.
4. You're walking in the front door of the funeral home.
5. You enter the room where the friend's family are gathered around the coffin.
6. Walking to within ten feet of the coffin, you see the top is open.
7. Walking toward the coffin, five feet away, you can see the dead person's face, very pale and powdery looking.
8. Two friends escort you up to the coffin to view the body.
9. As you stand within three feet of the coffin, you can see the dead man's face clearly, and you can hardly recognize him as your friend.
10. Standing there viewing the body, your two friends leave to greet some new arrivals.
11. Stepping closer to the coffin, you can see that the dead man looks much older and thinner than when you last saw him alive.
12. Stepping still closer, you reach out and touch the cold metal of the coffin.
13. Standing right beside the coffin, you reach down and touch the dead man's hand. It feels very cold.
14. You look intently at the dead man's face and try to remember how he looked when he was alive.
15. You leave the room looking for a water fountain, and enter a room with three open coffins in it.
16. As you reach the middle of the room, you see there are dead people in each of the coffins.
17. Looking around, you realize that you're alone in a room with three dead people.

FEAR OF STRANGERS

1. You're walking down the street with a friend when someone comes up to ask directions.

2. You're standing on a street corner when a bum walks up and asks you for a cigarette.

3. Upon entering a friend's home, you notice that two of the people there are strangers.

4. Your friend introduces you to the strangers and walks away.

5. You're at a large party talking to two good friends when three (five, eight, ten) strangers join your group.

6. As you continue talking with this group of three (five, eight, ten) strangers, you notice one (both) of your friends has moved to another group.

7. You're riding on a bus when the man sitting next to you strikes up a conversation.

8. You enter a friend's home and discover she has also invited 10 (20, 30, 50) people you've never seen before.

9. Your friend escorts you around introducing you to each of the strangers.

10. After the introductions, your friend excuses herself and leaves the room.

11. Upon entering your friend's home, you look around at 40 or 50 people and you don't see anyone you know.

12. You walk into a private club and realize you don't know anyone there.

13. As you enter a room full of strangers, everyone stops talking and turns to look at you.

appendix 2
checklist for self-directed systematic desensitization

SYSTEMATIC DESENSITIZATION CHECKLIST

Name _____   Date _____

Specific Fear Response _____

    Tasks   Date

1. Achieved skill in deep muscle relaxation   _____

2. Developed systematic desensitization hierarchy   _____

3. Checked hierarchy and made suggested or needed changes   _____

4. Developed ability to visualize scenes   _____

5. Record of systematic desensitization. Directions: Write the date and number of the session in the far left column, the number of the scene being visualized in the second column, and the number of times the scene was visualized in the third column. Record one scene per line. Indicate the level of discomfort produced during each visualization of any specific scene by writing in a number from 0 to 100 in the column on the far right. Zero means no discomfort, 100 means the highest degree of discomfort. Note: Each scene should be imagined enough times so that on its last visualization it produces *no* feeling of discomfort, or one no greater than *five* suds.

Date and Session Number	Scene Number	Number of Visualizations	Discomfort Level During Each Visualization (0 to 100 suds)

appendix 3
suggested readings

SUGGESTED READINGS

Self-control

Foster, C. *Developing self-control.* Kalamazoo: Behaviordelia, 1975.

Mahoney, M. J., & Thoresen, C. E. *Self-control: Power to the person.* Monterey: Brooks/Cole, 1974.

Thoresen, C. E., & Mahoney, M. J. *Behavioral self-control.* New York: Holt, Rinehart, & Winston, 1974.

Watson, D. L., & Tharp, R. C. *Self-directed behavior: Self-modification for personal adjustment.* Monterey: Brooks/Cole, 1972.

Williams, R. L., & Lang, J. D. *Toward a self-managed life style.* Boston: Houghton Mifflin, 1975.

Systematic Desensitization and Behavior Therapy

Dawley, H. H., & Wenrich, W. W. *Achieving assertive behavior: A guide to assertive training.* Monterey: Brooks/Cole, 1976.

Franks, C. M. (Ed.) *Behavior therapy: Appraisal and status.* New York: McGraw-Hill, 1969.

Lazarus, A. A. *Behavior therapy and beyond.* New York: McGraw-Hill, 1971.

O'Leary, K. D., & Wilson, G. T. *Behavior therapy: Application and outline.* Englewood Cliffs: Prentice-Hall, 1975.

Rimm, D. C., & Masters, J. C. *Behavior therapy: Techniques and empirical findings.* New York: Academic Press, 1974.

Wenrich, W. W. *A primer on behavior modification.* Monterey: Brooks/Cole, 1970.

Wolpe, J. *Psychotherapy by reciprocal inhibition.* Stanford: Stanford University Press, 1958.

Wolpe, J. *The practice of behavior therapy* (2nd ed.). New York: Pergamon Press, 1973.

Wolpe, J., & Lazarus, A. A. *Behavior therapy techniques: A guide to the treatment of neuroses.* New York: Pergamon Press, 1966.

Yates, A. J. *Behavior therapy.* New York: John Wiley & Sons, 1970.

ADDITIONAL BEHAVIORDELIA PRODUCTS OF INTEREST

DEVELOPING SELF-CONTROL
Carol Foster / 1974 / soft cover / 144 pages / 6 x 9

". . . The ultimate application of these techniques is by the behavior modifier to his own behavior. What Foster offers is a recipe for that application. She covers, clearly and concisely, the steps toward behavioral self-control. Extraneous material on theory, ethics, scientific basis, etc., is quite reasonably ignored. This is a cookbook, designed to teach the methods of self-control through the methods of behavior modification in a "programmed learning" fashion. It takes the reader through the method in many small, often repeated and reinforced steps."

AAAS Science Books and Films, May, 1975

CHILD PSYCHOLOGY: A BEHAVIORAL APPROACH
TO EVERYDAY PROBLEMS
Roger W. McIntire / 1975 / hard cover / 288 pages / 6 x 9

"Roger McIntire believes that people should not be allowed to wander blindly into the business of child-rearing. He has even advocated the licensing of parents (see 'Parenthood Training or Mandatory Birth Control: Take Your Choice,' *PT,* October, 1973). *Child Psychology* ... is his own guide to the nurture of the young. It could be used either as a text in the parenthood training he advocates or as a guide for harried parents. [It] was originally published by CRM Books as *For Love of Children.* The new edition is sprinkled liberally with case histories in which parents solve family problems with a dose of behavior modification."

Psychology Today, August, 1975

CONTINGENCY MANAGEMENT IN EDUCATION
AND OTHER EQUALLY EXCITING PLACES . . .
Richard W. Malott and Patricia Hartlep / 1972 / soft cover / 260 pages / 8½ x 11

"This zany, engaging comic book is actually a fine elementary text on applied behavioral principles. While directed at undergraduate psychology students, apparently, the book contains information a practicing physician may find useful, or entertaining, or both. Learn how Behaviorwoman helped a repulsive hippy to diet. Marvel how Captain Con Man steered a procrastinating graduate student through his PhD thesis. See how Behaviorman got rotten kids to read. And lots, lots more folks."

Practical Psychology for Physicians, May, 1975

RESPONSE COUNTER
This instrument takes the guesswork out of measuring behavior. Ideal for laboratory, class, clinic, or home use. You don't have to be a scientist to use one. If you're trying to change some personal behavior use the counter to keep track of your good moves — smiling — or your bad ones — smoking, overeating, swearing. You'll find the counter handy and easy to use. You can wear it like a watch or detach it from its strap for a pocket or a chain. Upper digits read from zero to 99, and the lower digit independent knob reads from zero to 9 for a total register of 999. A great aid for anyone collecting data. Beats moving marbles from pocket to pocket! **Discount available for multiple purchases.**

Send requests for additional information and/or catalogue to Behaviordelia, Inc. / PO Box 1044 / Department SD / Kalamazoo, Michigan 49005.